USING CHRISTIAN CONTEMPLATIVE PRACTICE WITH CHILDREN

by the same author

Listening to Young Children in Early Years Settings
A Practical Guide
Sonia Mainstone-Cotton
ISBN 978 1 78592 469 9
eISBN 978 1 78450 855 5

Promoting Emotional Wellbeing in Early Years Staff
A Practical Guide for Looking after Yourself and Your Colleagues
Sonia Mainstone-Cotton
ISBN 978 1 78592 335 7
eISBN 978 1 78450 656 8

Promoting Young Children's Emotional Health and Wellbeing
A Practical Guide for Professionals and Parents
Sonia Mainstone-Cotton
ISBN 978 1 78592 054 7
eISBN 978 1 78450 311 6

Can I tell you about Bipolar Disorder?
A Guide for Friends, Family and Professionals
Sonia Mainstone-Cotton
Illustrated by Jon Birch
ISBN 978 1 78592 470 5
eISBN 978 1 78450 854 8

USING CHRISTIAN CONTEMPLATIVE PRACTICE WITH CHILDREN

A Guide to Helping Children Explore Stillness and Meditation in Worship

Sonia Mainstone-Cotton

Jessica Kingsley *Publishers*
London and Philadelphia

First published in 2019
by Jessica Kingsley Publishers
73 Collier Street
London N1 9BE, UK
and
400 Market Street, Suite 400
Philadelphia, PA 19106, USA

www.jkp.com

Library of Congress Cataloging in Publication Data
A CIP catalog record for this book is available from the Library of Congress

British Library Cataloguing in Publication Data
A CIP catalogue record for this book is available from the British Library

ISBN 978 1 78592 662 4
eISBN 978 1 78592 663 1

Printed and bound in Great Britain

MIX
Paper from
responsible sources
FSC® C013604

Thank you

Ian and Gail, Tony, Will, Esther, Father Christopher, Mother Sarah and Flic: thank you all for your time, wisdom and kindness in this project. For all who were part of Sanctuary, thank you for the learning, exploring and creativity; this book could never have happened without that start. Iain, together we have explored contemplative practice, thank you for being my companion on this journey.

CONTENTS

INTRODUCTION

This book is about exploring Christian contemplative practice, mindfulness and stillness practice with children. There are a growing number of books looking at Christian spirituality, Christian mindfulness and contemplative practice for adults; this has partly come about due to the realisation that mental illness is a huge issue in our society. Within the secular world, mindfulness has been recognised to be very beneficial to adults' and children's wellbeing; it can help mental health, as the stillness practice that mindfulness draws on is good for our minds and bodies. Some in the church have been nervous or uncomfortable about mindfulness and stillness or contemplative practice, believing there are links between these and Eastern religions. However, scholars such as Richard Rohr, Ian Adams, Martin Laird, Thomas Merton and Benignus O'Rourke, all of whom I reference in this book, have been reminding us that contemplative stillness practice is a long-held tradition within Christianity, linking back to the time of the Desert Mothers and Fathers. In many parts of the church in the UK we have lost the link to this ancient practice; instead, so often our prayer lives can be about sending God a list of requests, praying for things to happen. O'Rourke (2011) suggests a prayer of stillness is about being with God without an agenda; the emphasis is just on being there.

There is a growing recognition that the church needs to re-engage with these old practices with adults, however there are very few voices about using these practices with children. I have worked with children for 30 years; I am passionate about how we can make a difference in their lives. For the last 21 years I have been exploring how we can use silence and quiet, contemplative practice with children; I have used these practices with families in the home, in church, and within early years and education. So much of our work with children both in church and in education is often busy, loud and rushed. So often our worship times in churches are noisy, full and wordy. I firmly believe we need to relearn how to sit with silence, how to have a time of quiet and stillness and how to hear God in the stillness – and we need to teach these skills to children.

This book is about offering some ideas for using stillness practice with children, finding silence and hearing God in the stillness. The ideas are all from practice that I have tried and been involved in with children. This book starts from the assumption that children of all ages are able to engage and have a relationship with God. Karen Marie Yust (2004) encourages us to acknowledge that all ages are able to engage in a faith with God. This book is not going to explore at what age children can engage; I believe all children can engage and that it is the role of the adult to support and model that engagement. I firmly believe that if we are leading these practices with children, then we as adults also need to be engaging in them.

When we consider contemplative practice and children it is often thought the two cannot go together. From my experience, I know that we can help children to find moments of stillness. However, sometimes children will be wriggly, make the odd noise or ask a question in the middle of a practice. This is okay: the aim is to encourage the idea of finding some calmness and stillness but not to be authoritarian about it. Children will be children; they will sometimes be bouncy and curious and playful, but they can also appreciate and engage with calmness and quiet. I also want to encourage you to think about this as an inclusive resource. The ideas and suggestions work across all ages and abilities. Some of the most beautiful moments of stillness and contemplative worship I have encountered have been in services with children and adults with learning disabilities. Yes, there were some noises and movements but everyone in their own way, with support, was able to engage in moments of stillness.

The first section of the book offers some thoughts around how we work with children in churches, children's wellbeing and the church history around contemplative practice. It includes interviews with a variety of people who work with children and young people and others who are firmly rooted in the contemplative tradition. The second section of the book offers a wide variety of practices that you can carry out with children and young people. I offer suggestions around the appropriate age for each activity, although these are broad and not prescriptive; you know your children so use these as a rough guide. The ideas are not prescriptive either, but they suggest ways you could engage and support children in each practice. When using these ideas I encourage you to try them for yourself first.

I hope that you will tweak and add to them, making them your own.

If contemplative practice is new to you, I hope you find some ideas and thoughts that will help in your own spiritual life and in the way you support children. This book has many references to some excellent writers on this subject; I encourage you to continue reading further and discover these writers and enjoy their insights. If contemplative practice is a well-experienced path for you, I hope this book helps you find ways to share this wonderful practice with children.

My hope is that you will find a glimmer of ideas and ways to help children with contemplative practice, as I believe there is so much within it to enhance both children's and adults' mental wellbeing.

REFERENCES

O'Rourke, B. (2011) *Finding Your Hidden Treasure: The Way of Silent Prayer.* London: Darton, Longman and Todd.
Yust, K.M. (2004) *Real Kids, Real Faith.* San Franscisco, CA: Jossey-Bass.

Section 1

Children, Church and the Contemplative Tradition

CHAPTER 1

THE CHURCH'S WORK WITH CHILDREN

This chapter is going to look at the different ways many churches currently work with children and briefly explore the history of this. However, to start this chapter I probably need to be clear about where I am coming from. I have worked with children for 30 years, in churches, in schools, in early years settings, within charities and early on in my career as a nanny. I currently work as a freelance trainer, a writer and a nurture consultant. At the heart of all my practice is a child-centred approach. To explain what I mean by this, the following are the three simple questions I ask myself when engaging with children:

1. What are the children interested in?

2. How will this work for the children?

3. What are the children telling us through their words, non-verbal language and behaviour?

These questions help to guide all my work and underpin the suggestions in this book.

WHY DID THE CHURCH START WORKING WITH CHILDREN?

The church has a long tradition of teaching children. This started in Britain in the 1780s, when Sunday schools were originally set up by Christian philanthropists to enable children to learn to read and write. By the mid-19th century most children went to Sunday school in the UK, where they were largely taught to read from the Bible and were taught Bible verses (Larson 2008).

In 1902 the Anglican Church was caused to rethink how it worked with children: a Canadian named Hamilton Archibald encouraged Sunday school teachers to have the child at the centre of their teaching and to think about how they could approach Bible teaching, focusing on how the child viewed the world and what their experiences were (Sutcliffe 2001). Some of the key messages from Archibald back in 1902 are really relevant for us today. I find myself cheering as I read them:

All education needs to begin with the child.

We need to recognise children's love of nature.

Teach children through their senses.

I'd suggest this is not only relevant for how we work with children in churches but also within our wider education system too. These are so similar to messages I have been giving to teachers and educators throughout my career.

Questions for reflection

Take a moment to consider the statements above and think about the children's work you are involved in.

- How much of your work is child centred? Use my three questions at the beginning of the chapter to help you think about this.

- How much of your work is based on what the children are interested in and curious about? Do you know what excites and interests the children in your groups?

- How do you use nature and all our senses in your work with children?

THE CHURCH BEGINS TO THINK ABOUT ALL-AGE SERVICES AND THE CHURCH AS ONE FAMILY

In the 1940s it was beginning to be recognised that many children were going to Sunday schools but were then stopping at around the age of 10 and were not becoming adults in the church. A minister called H.A. Hamilton helped to rethink and challenge the views of the church about children. He advocated the need for children to feel that being part of a church was similar to being part of a family. He was really concerned that many of the adults in churches did not really know the children in the Sunday schools. He asked questions around whether the adults really understood what it was like to be a child at that time; whether they knew what concerned children, interested and excited them. Did the adults really know how life was for a child (Sutcliffe 2001)? I was really fascinated to read this from the 1940s as these are exactly the questions I ask of church workers now; I find there is something really encouraging about knowing what people years ago were asking about and advocating these same ideas. Hamilton was a big advocate of all-age services and children being actively involved in them, and through his influence there began to be a move towards all-age services.

CHILDREN'S WORK NOW

It is very common now for children who go to church to go out to their children's groups either at the beginning or part way through the church service to have their own learning sessions. This has developed over the years and there are many programmes and teaching guides to help people run these groups.

Over the years these groups, particularly the children's groups, have often focused on games, loud songs, Bible stories, colouring-in sheets and entertainment. At some recent training that I was delivering to children's workers in churches I asked why so much of the children's work in churches is loud, bouncy and energetic. Some of the reflections from people were:

'There is a feeling we need to show that Jesus and God are cool.'

'Adults think that is what children want.'

'Adults are scared that if it is not entertaining, children won't like it and then the numbers will fall.'

'If children like church then they might stay into adulthood.'

In my research for this book I spent time looking at websites and books about worship with children. I found one website which gave *68 reasons why children's ministry matters.*[1] Two of their suggestions were as follows:

> *It is fun for children, God invented fun:* I read this as suggesting that the majority of our work with children needs to be fun, fun, fun.

> *It helps children want to come to church:* this is an interesting idea, and I think it links with the sometimes held view that children's work in churches is about bums on seats in later life.

An often, long-held view of working with children, particularly in church work, has been that we need to be preparing/training children for some future life as an adult. I have huge issues with this view; I strongly believe that we need to be listening to where the child is now, and recognising that a child has rights and views and needs now, and our role is to support them in the here and now. Church workers have often told me that they presume children want lots of noise, excitement and entertainment; however in my experience, when we stop and listen to children we often hear and see very different wants, concerns and questions. I wonder if some of our energy-driven, noise-driven worship comes out of adults' fear of silence? To spend time in silence can be very scary for some; it is in times of silence that sometimes we encounter our own insecurities.

---

[1]   https://ministry-to-children.com/benefits

Questions for reflection

Take a moment to think about how you do children's work in your church or school. What model do you use? Think about what has influenced your practice.

- Are you using a style you experienced as a child?
- Are you using a style that you think or know children want – how do you know?
- Have you involved the children you work with in conversations about the style you use?

EDUCATING CHILDREN

When Sunday schools were first started their main role was to teach children to read and write. This was at a time before school was compulsory and when many children were working. The main aim of much of the children's work in churches now is to tell children about Jesus: when they are younger to teach them about Bible stories and as they grow older to encourage a discipline of reading the Bible and having a relationship with God.

There are many ways this can happen. I am going to look at a few of these in the following sections.

USING BIBLE STORIES, CRAFT AND GAMES

This has grown to be a very popular way of teaching children. For younger children, it often involves reading or telling a Bible story and using craft materials to make something representing the story. There are many different lesson plans from many different organisations, all using an adaptation of this style of work. For adults who are leading the children's work, it provides a lot of resources and is an easy way to deliver this work without having to spend much time planning. The plans often involve acting out parts of the story and spending time talking with the children about the story. For example, in the parable of the lost sheep, this could mean reading the story, making sheep with a template, acting out the story, playing a lost sheep game, discussing why Jesus told the story, asking who the sheep are, and discussing how Jesus loves us all and how we are all valuable. This style can be adapted for different ages, for instance by providing more discussion for older children and differentiating activities across the ages.

There are many resources to offer ideas for this type of work. Scripture Union[2] have some free resources and Roots[3] also provide some free ideas. I particularly like the range that Urban Saints[4] provide as they offer a wide range of resources that also link well to contemporary culture and look at wider concerns; for example, they have a section on handling emotions with lesson plans, activities both high energy and calming, links to Bible verses and what insights can be gained from the Bible in relation to these. Bible story craft is mainly used for primary-aged children (4–11 years).

CONCERNS AROUND THE TEMPLATE/CRAFT MODEL

My one concern with many of these resources is the template model a lot of them use. Alongside writing I work as an

---

[2]   https://content.scriptureunion.org.uk

[3]   www.rootsontheweb.com/about-roots/what-is-roots

[4]   www.energize.uk.net

early years nurture consultant and trainer; my specialism is early years, wellbeing and listening to children. In my work life, I advocate following children's ideas using in the moment planning, which is about following a child's interest and using that in planning, and using many creative ways to work with children. I have written a book about how and why we listen to young children (Mainstone-Cotton 2019). Through my writing, training and direct work I encourage people to move away from the template model. So I find it very challenging and frustrating when I see children in church colouring in sheets of Jesus and lambs or following a step-by-step guide on how to make a sheep. I believe there are other ways! This isn't a criticism aimed at church children's workers, as I understand that many are giving their time for free, are often short on time and may not be trained educators and so using a ready model can be very helpful. However, I am critical at the organisations that are making these and would like to challenge some of their practice. I do believe it is possible to help children to be creative without using templates, even if the adults don't feel creative, by providing some open-ended resources, for example, paper, pens, wool, glue and grass. You could still invite children to make something that was linked to the story, for example, the lost sheep story, without being controlling and directive, and if children choose to make a dinosaur instead, that is fine! Or you could introduce a story and then enable the children to explore this through different open-ended activities or stations; for example, craft items, small world play (playing with figures, animals etc.), LEGO® or block play, sand play, sensory play using dried rice and so on. The bonus of using this style is that apart from the initial set up of the room, this is not heavily reliant on adult support. Individual children can choose the things that interest them and can follow their own ideas and be as creative as they want. This also allows children to be calm, in the moment and focused with their playing; it often encourages a quietness and focus. Adults can then support the children's explorations by coming alongside them and finding out what they are doing. You can all come together at the end and talk about what you have been doing. At the end of the book, I offer further suggestions on how you can open up children's work without using templates.

HOW WE COMMUNICATE WITH CHILDREN AND LISTEN TO CHILDREN

I have been hugely inspired over the years by the work in Reggio Emilia, a small northern town in Italy, which has full-time artists working with children in preschools. They firmly believe that children are citizens now and that we need to listen to their ideas and their concerns now. Our work with children is about recognising their own unique place at this moment. Their approach embeds creativity and the recognition that children express themselves through a hundred different languages (Edwards, Gandini and Forman 1998). This phrase is about recognising that children express themselves in many different ways, through dance, singing, drawing, playing, modelling, sitting, running. The role of adults is to tune in and recognise how children are expressing themselves, and meet children where they are at. I love this worldview and I feel it offers some insight to us in churches. I believe it expresses how

God communicates with us; God sees us where we are, and speaks to us through many different means, meeting us in a way that works for us. I worry that sometimes we miss this in the church, particularly through our children's work. If our model of working is a formula, template, programme-driven, one-model way, we may be missing out on how we communicate with children and young people (and adults!). I do believe we could learn a lot for our children's work from the many creative ways high-quality early years practitioners are working with children. We need to learn to stop and ask, find out what children think and what their views are, find out what excites them and worries them and use this in our work with them. At the heart of this is relational work; Tony Cook refers to relational work in our interview below. Dr Howard Worsley (2009) talks about how much we can learn from children when we stop and listen to them. He writes about how we can learn about how a child sees God when we explore the Bible with them and listen to their ideas and thoughts. These excellent ways of working can then be adapted to work across the ages. I further explore ways of working creatively with children in my book on children's wellbeing (Mainstone-Cotton 2017).

Example from practice

I have a friend called Will (I have included an interview with him in Chapter 2). In his work life he is a child counsellor and he also runs the children's work in his church with his wife Esther. They start all their sessions by simply checking in how the children are and what is going on in their lives. He believes that unless they know what is going on for the children, and unless they have connected with them, they can't expect the children to jump into and join in with the arranged activity. If it turns out some of the children have had a difficult week, they will adapt and change their plans and give the children the chance to talk and be listened to. They also have a tent in the room. This is a space where children can take themselves off to have some time by themselves and then join the group when they are ready. The adults will support children appropriately to feel safe in this group. The adults running this group are emotionally literate and aware of the importance of emotional support for the children.

USING DISCUSSIONS LINKED WITH CONTEMPORARY CULTURE

This style is most commonly used with senior-aged children (11–18 years), again using games and sometimes making activities. My experience is that often the workers with the older age range – and often the resources available for the older children – are more creative and imaginative and link with contemporary culture. I also think it is more common for workers with this age group to ask their group what they want to do and what they are interested in. I have seen some excellent resources linking to current films, enabling the group to use these to explore together issues around faith, belief and worldview.

For this book, I have interviewed people who work with children or are involved in contemplative practice in the church. One of these is Tony Cook. Tony has worked for Bath and Wells Diocese for 19 years and heads up the children and youth work. My interview with him was about how we currently deliver children and youth work in churches and he had some really useful insights. He suggests that youth work is often relational based. I personally think this is a really important style and one that could be adapted for children's work. My questions and a summary of his answers follow.

INTERVIEW WITH TONY COOK ABOUT CHURCHES WORKING WITH CHILDREN AND YOUNG PEOPLE

WHY IS THE CHURCH WORKING WITH CHILDREN AND YOUNG PEOPLE?

The church is one of the last intergenerational organisations within society. It is one of the few places we can have 2-year-olds and 80-year-olds at the same place, and the church really needs to value this.

Also, the church is informed by scriptures such as Mark 10 'let the children come to me' or Psalm 78 'pass the faith onto the next generation'; this gives it a theological underpinning for the generational church. The Sunday School Movement started in the 1780s to help educate poor children who had to work and who had no access to other forms of education, and this enriched and transformed the lives of generations of children. Today, Sunday schools and other forms of children's ministry are different, but they are no less important as they enable churches to reach out to children, young people and families in their communities.

WHY DO YOU THINK WE HAVE THE CURRENT MODEL IN CHURCHES; FOR EXAMPLE, CHILDREN IN FOR 10 MINUTES AND THEN OUT TO THEIR OWN GROUPS?

I think this about adults trying to create appropriate activities for children, rather than thinking creatively about how we can do intergenerational church appropriately and well. Our liturgy/language and styles of worship over the years have become mostly exclusive for adults. This has made it hard for children to remain in the same space as adults and they often become bored. Rather than churches thinking what we can do that embraces all ages, many churches simply provide a different space for children and adults. I acknowledge that it is really hard to do intergenerational, all-age worship well; I also believe it is okay to have separate spaces and operate separate conversations and teaching, but if the sole aim is to get the children out of the way, I don't believe that models the body of the church as God intended. The issue of the separate spaces is often adult organised and children are rarely asked what they want and how it could work for them. If we asked this, we might see a different picture.

WHY IS MOST OF THE CHILDREN'S WORK IN CHURCHES USING THE MODEL OF BIBLE STORIES, LOUD SINGING, GAMES, CRAFT?

I think there are some significant differences in children's ministry and youth ministry. Children's ministry is often centred around programmes that use Bible stories, singing, games and crafts, whilst youth ministry is less 'programme' driven and much more relational focused. It also invariably involves huge amounts of food.

In children's ministry, I think it is this way because it offers a structure for the children and a framework for those running children's ministry. Sometimes this can appear to entertain the children whilst the adults get on with their worship, but I don't think that is the intention. Some churches use programmes really well and include times when the children have amazing opportunities to sit still and reflect. However, I do think the programme remains the driver in many forms of children's ministry. There are beautiful examples of children's ministry, such as Godly Play, that are not programme driven, but even Godly Play has a structure that focuses on a script.

Youth ministry on the other hand is much more about investing in the relationship with young people and providing a safe and appropriate space where they can talk about issues and concerns and how this relates to God and faith. This is much less programme driven and offers more space to discuss, debate and be reflective. It can also provide opportunities for young people to share their thoughts and ideas, which is more important to them than any structured programme.

I get that the vast majority of adults running both children and youth ministry are giving their time for free and an 'off-the-shelf' programme can be a life saver for busy volunteers. It also provides a structure and guidance that many value. So I am not knocking the use of all programmes. However, I wonder if we can move away from the entertaining style programmes and adopt a more relational model approach in both youth and children's ministry. This could enable both youth and children's leaders to get alongside their groups and help them to discover where God really relates in their lives.

I also feel we need to explore more contemplative times with both children and young people and allow much more space for silence and reflection. This requires fewer organised and structured activities, which might be a bit scarier for the adult leaders. However, it might also create more space for God to speak through the children and young people as they listen, reflect and discuss. I do believe things are beginning to change in many churches and leaders are beginning to rely less on programmes, but maybe we need to be brave and go even further.

SO IF YOUTH WORK IS OFTEN RELATIONAL BASED, WHY IS CHILDREN'S WORK DIFFERENT?

I think this is largely down to fears around safeguarding and how we appropriately interact with younger children. There may also be time factors, especially on a Sunday morning during worship. However, for some it might simply be the fear of stepping away from traditional models of children's ministry and that is how we have always done it.

Taking all these factors into account and with good practice in place, I think we could do some amazing relational stuff and contemplative stuff with very young children, in a similar way to what we might do with young people. This will require better understanding, different approaches and some tips on how we might do it. Hopefully, this book will massively help with this. We may also need a bank of questions that explore the wonder of God and faith with children, like Godly Play does with stories.

If we do, it might help some churches to move away from the safety of programmes and better use the time spent with children to simply get alongside them, listen to them and find out how they view the world and God.

There is no doubt some churches are already doing this stuff really well and we need to learn from them. I also know this type of thinking may not be for everyone, and that is okay.

MY REFLECTIONS

I found interviewing Tony really useful, particularly his reflection on the difference between programme-driven work with children and often relational-driven work with teenagers. It helped me to reflect that so much of my direct work with children and young people over the years has been relational across the ages. I firmly believe that as a church we have an important part to play in finding out what excites and worries children; we need to be a safe place for them where they can truly be themselves and learn that they are loved by God. As Tony says we need, of course, to make sure that we have exemplary safeguarding practice around this. But in the same way that a good school teacher really knows the children in their class, the adults in churches should really know the children they are working with, really understand what excites them, what worries them, how they learn and what works for them. Of course, many churches will have adults working with children on a rota basis, but there is no reason why a church couldn't adopt the excellent early years practice of a key person approach, allocating one adult to a few children in the group whose job is to really know those children. They could find out what those children love and hate, how they like to spend their time and so on, and then share that information with the rest of the group in the planning meeting.

ALL-AGE SERVICES

As I mentioned above, in the 1940s A.H. Hamilton believed that churches should be like a family and worshipping together, across the ages, should be a regular part of the church life. Often now, children are included in parts of church services and sometimes there are specific all-age services. Many of the resources for children's work also offer ideas and templates for all-age services. Over the years I have seen many churches struggle with doing all-age services well; so often they can involve games, loud action songs, entertainment and storytelling in an attempt to engage the children. However, they often don't engage children and don't engage the adults either. I have heard many people complain about all-age services in churches. I think one of the challenges is moving away from the idea that we need to entertain children in church. It is unusual to see children encouraged to join in with times of quiet, contemplation, meditation and stillness. I think we are often worried as adults that children will be bored or cannot engage in these practices. However, my experience is that they can; with support they can be involved.

Over the years I have been involved in exploring how to embed and embrace all-age worship in a way that works across the ages. For 16 years I co-led an alternative worship community called Sanctuary. All our services were all age; we used a participative model encouraging an active engagement by all. The participative, curatorial model was a common thread in alternative worship communities in the 2000s and in Sanctuary we felt that it worked really well across the ages. We often talked about how a good Pixar film worked for children, teens and adults in the way it was layered. We aimed to layer our services and participation elements in this same way. In Sanctuary we would often use times of reflection, stillness and meditation, and children would always be part of this. For over 10 years, we were involved in leading all-age alternative worship services at Greenbelt. One year we led a service with around 200 people of all ages attending and as part of this we led a guided meditation. The person leading spoke the words and there were images relating to the words on a screen. We explained to the children that we were listening to the words, listening to God and watching the pictures. For five minutes there was silence, apart from the words being spoken. We had toddlers and preschoolers, primary aged and teenagers, parents and grandparents, all quietly meditating, praying and being contemplative together. It was beautiful.

STILLNESS AND CONTEMPLATIVE PRACTICE

Before I started this book I did a small piece of research to explore examples of different stillness and contemplative practice that were happening across different denominations and with different ages of children. The main examples shared were examples of small moments of practice:

- having a moment of silence at the end of a session
- using reflective colour sheets from Premier
- sitting and listening to calming music
- sitting with some quiet, having a candle to look at
- using meditations
- using Lectio Devina.

Most of these examples were with older children.

Mark Yaconelli has written a few books encouraging the use of contemplative practice with young people and these are excellent (Yaconelli 2006; 2010). I think these have been very influential for many youth workers. At the start of his book *Contemplative Youth Ministry,* he suggests that we don't know how to be with our kids, with the emphasis on the just 'being'. He suggests that we know how to entertain, test and quiz them but we don't know how to be with them. His writing is aimed at those working with young people; however, I would extend this to those working with younger children too. I feel we need to relearn how to be, how to listen, how to sit with children and hear God. Maybe as adults we need to learn first how to be, how to sit with God in the quiet space, how to learn to 'Be still and know that I am God' (Psalm 46).

The rest of this book is going to explore what contemplative practice is and how we can use this with children. I am also going to look at why I think embracing contemplative practice is so important for both children and adults, and how I feel the church has much to offer in this area.

REFERENCES

Edwards, C., Gandini, L. and Forman, G. (1998) *The Hundred Languages of Children: The Reggio Emilia Approach – Advanced Reflections.* London: Ablex Publishing.

Larson, T. (2008) When did Sundays schools start? Accessed on 14/01/2019 at www.christianitytoday.com/history/2008/august/when-did-sunday-schools-start.html

Mainstone-Cotton, S. (2017) *Promoting Young Children's Emotional Health and Wellbeing: A Practical Guide for Professionals and Parents.* London: Jessica Kingsley Publishers.

Mainstone-Cotton, S. (2019) *Listening to Young Children in Early Years Settings: A Practical Guide*. London. Jessica Kingsley Publishers.

Sutcliffe, J. (2001) *Tuesday's Child: A Reader for Christian Educators*. Birmingham: Christian Education Publications.

Worsley, H. (2009) *A Child Sees God: Children Talk about Bible Stories*. London: Jessica Kingsley Publishers.

Yaconelli, M. (2006) *Contemplative Youth Ministry: Practising the Presence of Jesus with Young People*. London. SPCK.

Yaconelli, M. (2010) *Wonder, Fear and Longing: A Book of Prayers*. London: SPCK.

CHAPTER 2

WHY CHILDREN NEED TO LEARN STILLNESS AND CONTEMPLATIVE PRACTICE

WELLBEING

I spend a lot of my working life thinking about, writing about and supporting children's wellbeing. I work part-time as a freelance nurture consultant for a small team in Bath called the Nurture Outreach Service, part of a small charity called Brighter Futures. In this role I support children, mainly 4-year-olds who need additional help in their transition to school. I spend a lot of time with children who have a low wellbeing; for a variety reasons they are finding life and the transition to school very hard and extremely scary. This role has taught me so much about the importance of good wellbeing. I have spent many hours researching wellbeing and how to help children and adults to have good wellbeing (Mainstone-Cotton 2017a; 2017b). We know that in the UK poor mental health is a serious concern for children, teenagers and adults. Many of the children you encounter will be struggling with their mental health.

Current statistics are that 10 per cent of children have a diagnosable mental illness; it is believed that in a class of 30 children in the 5–16 age range, three will have a mental health problem. These are the children that have been diagnosed, although many will also be suffering from mental health issues that have not been diagnosed. One in four adults will experience a mental illness at some point every year. Through all my research and practice I have observed three common threads and I am now going to briefly look at each of these.

PRESSURE

We live in a culture where, as adults, we are often under a huge amount of pressure. The cost of living is rising, there is stress from work or job uncertainty and many people have problems with housing and financial concerns. There is also increased pressure on our children: we are testing children earlier and earlier in schools, we talk about achievement all the time and children also feel increasingly under pressure via social media. The current craze amongst many primary and lower senior school-aged children is an online video game called *Fortnite*. Although in many ways this isn't an overly violent game, it is very competitive and children playing it can feel under a huge amount of pressure to reach the number one slot out of the 100 players they are competing against. The games are short but intense, and can give rise to strong feelings for the player. Added to this is the issue of the number of hours children play the game for. If we constantly feel under pressure it can lead to high levels of stress and distress. It can lead to feelings of helplessness and despair. Do we want this for our children?

BUSY LIVES

The second issue is that we are so busy. How often, when someone has asked how you are, has your answer been 'I am so busy'? To be busy has almost become a badge of honour. Half of my working week is spent in schools, and a school is a hive of busyness. As I am writing this chapter, it is the end of the school year and for a whole variety of reasons it has been a particularly challenging term. I am pretty good at stopping, slowing down and looking after my wellbeing, but even I am desperate for the six-week school holiday! Being busy for a time is fine; the problem is when you are constantly busy, when we forget to slow down, when we don't stop. This is when our wellbeing is affected, and we become ill. This busyness does not just affect adults but children as well. Many middle-class children now live extremely busy lives, with a full and challenging day in school followed by after school clubs, and with some children attending after school activities daily – sometimes more than one each evening – and then having busy weekends. We have forgotten how to allow our children to stop, to be bored, to daydream. There is much evidence coming out showing us that children need to slow down and be less busy, or at least be less busy inside on devices and with pre-planned activities; being busy whilst playing and exploring outside is good for children's wellbeing. Richard Louv has a website called 'children and nature',[1] exploring the negative impact being busy inside has on children and the positive impact being outside has. I believe there is a skill in learning how to slow down, how

---

[1]   www.childrenandnature.org/about

to be slow, how to stop. It is a skill that many adults have lost and have forgotten how to do. If this is the case then we cannot teach it to our children.

NOISE

The third common strand is around noise. We mostly live in very noisy environments: there is often noise around us from traffic; we have radios/TVs on in the background; lots of young children's toys make noises; and children spend a lot of time playing on tablets and phones making noise. We have forgotten how to sit with silence, so often we fill the space with noise. If as adults we don't know how to sit with silence, we can't teach this to children. We are often particularly guilty of this in churches. Many services are filled with noise, to the extent that even when a worship leader says, 'We are now going to have a time of silence' it is filled with background 'ambient' music or someone starts praying over the mic. I would suggest that in many churches we have lost the ability to sit with silence as it can make us feel very uncomfortable. I was recently in an Anglican Eucharist service. In many ways it was a lovely service, but it was back to back with words. Lots of words in the liturgy, singing, prayers, a sermon, liturgy for the communion. At the point in the service when communion was served, I breathed a sigh of relief believing there would finally be some silence, but then the guitarist started to play her guitar and sing. Sadly in the 1-hour 15-minute service there was no room for any silence, not even one minute.

Questions for reflection

- How busy is your life?
- How often do you slow down and stop?
- When did you last intentionally say 'I need to stop for this moment, I need to slow down'?
- When did you last sit in silence?

STILLNESS, SLOWNESS, CONTEMPLATION AND MENTAL HEALTH

Many GPs, mental health charities and the NHS are now advocating that people learn some stillness and meditation practice. It is also recommended by NICE as a preventive practice. This is often referred to as mindfulness; it has been recognised by health professionals as a very holistic way to support people and their mental health. This has largely been influenced by Jon Kabat-Zinn, who, in the 1970s, developed a mindfulness programme to support people with chronic pain. In the 1990s in the UK, Mark Williams and colleagues were influenced by Kabat-Zinn's programme and went on to develop a mindfulness programme with cognitive behavioural therapy (CBT) for patients with depression. They found this worked very effectively. Mark Williams (Williams and Penman 2011) went on to develop an 8-week programme for anyone to use, which is now delivered all over the UK. Evidence has shown that regular mindfulness practice can lower blood pressure and reduce stress levels. Brain scans have found that mindfulness practice can increase activity in the area of the brain which is linked to positive emotion, the pre-frontal cortex (Mental Health Foundation[2]). Mindfulness practice encourages being present, being in the moment and noticing what is happening within you and around you. It requires us to slow down; it requires quiet or silence within us. Tim Stead (2016), a former vicar in Oxford, teaches mindfulness and describes mindfulness practice as being more aware of your experience in the present moment in a non-judgemental way. Brian Draper (2017) describes how we can all have moments of mini awakenings, such as when we see a beautiful rainbow or a buzzard swoops in front of the car as we are driving. He describes these moments when we make a deeper connection with life as living with soul and suggests that mindfulness practice helps us to be more aware of these precious moments and has helped him to deepen his Christian faith. Some view mindfulness sceptically and see it as simply a new fad; others view it as a useful tool to help with their stress levels without really engaging in what is stressing them out. Draper suggests that mindfulness can help us to find moments to quiet our anxious and overactive minds and remember who we are and what we can be. I would take this further and say that within Christian practice, mindfulness helps us to get back in touch with the still voice that is within us, to re-engage with God in the stillness and silence.

The other recommendation of many GPs and health services is spending time outside, being in nature – walking in woods, for example. This practice often brings with it a quietness. There is growing evidence to show the positive impact these practices can have on people's mental health

---

[2]   www.mentalhealth.org.uk/a-to-z/m/mindfulness

and wellbeing. Florence Williams (2017) explores how being outside can positively affect our mental health. She looks at many different university research projects examining the impact that being outside has on our mental and physical wellbeing. Chiba University researchers found that a casual walk in a forest had a 12.7 per cent decrease on the participants' cortisol levels and a 103 per cent increase on the parasympathetic nervous activity, our relaxed state (Miyazaki 2012).

However, the area of mindfulness and spending time outside as part of a contemplative and worship practice has concerned and worried some in the church, with fears around links to Buddhism and Pantheism. In the next chapter, I am going to look more deeply at the long Christian tradition of stillness and contemplative practice, and using outdoor spaces as part of this. I will be showing how there is a link with this long tradition and what many today call mindfulness. I am aware that for some, including several of my friends, there is deep fear and concern that mindfulness is based in Eastern religions, for example Buddhism, and that can bring up many concerns. I will address these in the next chapter and refer to the long-held tradition of Christians in contemplative practice, stillness practice and meditations. Tim Stead (2016) suggests that mindfulness practices offer us a way to make space for God.

WHY CHILDREN BENEFIT FROM STILLNESS PRACTICE

As I mentioned earlier, many of our children are becoming increasingly stressed, anxious, mentally unwell and busy.

Most of my training and working practice is within early years, although I have a lot of experience of working across the ages. I firmly believe that if we can get things right in the early years – if we can teach younger children essential life skills – this will form a firm foundation for them to grow on from. Through my nurture role with 4-year-olds, I have seen and experienced the benefit of teaching young children moments of slowing down, being still, noticing what is happening in their bodies, being comfortable in stillness and silence. The children I work with are often very disregulated and stressed. They can quickly become agitated, very cross or overwhelmed. These children urgently need to learn calmness; they need to learn how to slow down, rest, find stillness and be comfortable in silence. If all children know is how to be busy, loud and excited, they are missing out on an essential life skill.

Many schools are now beginning to recognise the importance of teaching children these skills and there are many schools in the UK which are teaching mindfulness, using it as a daily practice. The Mindfulness in Schools Project[3] is used by a lot of schools in the UK and is part of a research project called the MYRIAD project[4], which is looking at children's resilience and mental health. Quaker schools often start the day with a meditation practice. Dr Noel Keating (2017), who worked in education for 40 years in Ireland and went on to develop the Meditation with Children project, advocates that there is an urgent need for silence and stillness in our modern world. He proposes that

---

[3]   https://mindfulnessinschools.org
[4]   www.myriadproject.org

meditation practice makes that possible and that this is a skill that should be taught in schools. Noel has helped create a mindfulness project used in schools in Ireland, based on Christian mindfulness/meditation practice. As part of Noel's research and practice with children, he interviewed 70 children from schools using the mindfulness project, asking the children for their comments on mindfulness. They reported the following (Keating 2017):

It helped them to let go of all the drama in their head.

It helped them to feel calmer, restored and relaxed.

It helped them to generate energy and confidence.

it helped them to make better decisions.

This work in schools is excellent; however, I have often felt that some of the church is being left behind. As a church we have a link with many children, through our church services, church schools, holiday clubs and community work. I really believe that as a church we can reach into our old traditions and draw out some guidance and wisdom around stillness and contemplative practice which would benefit many children and young people today. Keating (2017) suggests that meditation as a secular practice is seen as a tool for quietening the mind. He proposes that the wisdom from Christian traditions is to see it differently, seeing it instead as a way of helping us enter into the quiet that is already there. It is often suggested that one of the outcomes of the Christian tradition of contemplative, silent, mindful practice is that it helps us to become increasingly authentic and compassionate to the world, and more Christ centred. Christian meditation is different in the way it is Christ centred and recognises the connection between the human spirit and the Holy Spirit. Psalm 46:10: 'Be still and know that I am God' reminds us of the stillness and quietness that is already there. For me this is key; I firmly believe there is a quietness that we need to relearn and find, and I know we can help children to do this also.

OUR MISLED VIEWS AROUND CHILDREN AND STILLNESS

When I wrote my first book exploring how to support young children's wellbeing (Mainstone-Cotton 2017a), I asked many practitioners about their experience of using stillness practice with young children. I was writing this book in 2016 and the idea of using mindfulness and stillness practice within early years was still fairly new and not really embedded by many early years practitioners. In my initial discussions many people told me that young children could not be still or the times they could were often when they were listening to a story. But I knew from my experience of being a parent and from using contemplative stillness practice through our alternative worship community services (Sanctuary) that children were able to engage in times of stillness and times of silence. I believed the key was in how adults framed these times and supported children. Two years on, the early years community is becoming much more aware of the benefits of using stillness practice with young children, and there have been many books over the last few years on mindfulness and yoga practice with young children, and on teaching children breathing skills, ways to slow down and noticing and being present. However, I feel the church is still catching up on understanding this.

I believe that young children are naturally curious, interested and often mindful. My training is in early years and I have had the privilege of working with many young children over the years and have two of my own. When I first started working at 18, I nannied for two families who had flats in the same house. One family had two boys and the other had three boys. I learnt so much from these boys; I often walked to the local park with them – walking with under-5s is always an adventure! The 10-minute walk to the park always took far longer. There were sticks to pick up, snails to look at, poo to poke (with the sticks!), doorways to peer into, stone carved lions to find and stare at, bugs to find. They would stop and peer, and look and be still noticing their new-found treasures. These walks were mindful: they were slow, they were intentional and there were moments of stillness. I learnt from these boys there was no point in rushing; the walk was as interesting as the end destination, sometimes more interesting. I believe these are the beginnings of a child's ability to notice, to be still, to be mindful. If we can help children to hang onto those skills then we are equipping them well.

Stillness and silence practice is not always about physically being still. For some adults and children this is extremely difficult, but you can still help children find stillness through walking and some activity, as stillness is about finding an inner calm. At the end of the book I share a variety of ideas for practice; many are not based on sitting or lying still.

In the alternative worship community I jointly led, we often used a variety of stillness practices that children were part of. Some examples we used that you could try are given below. At the end of the book I explore these more and give some other examples of ones to try.

GUIDED MEDITATIONS

We had a variety of writers in our community and different members of the group would often write a meditation to use in our services. We always made sure these were short, around 7 to 10 minutes. We would have large cushions and blankets on the floor for people to lie on or sit on, and we also had images linked to the words, projected for people to see. We would introduce this by explaining that we were going to listen to some words and spend time listening to God. If people wanted to look at the pictures as well as the words, they could. The reader would slowly read the meditation while the images were projected. In our experience children always took part in this, in silence, looking and listening.

USING STATIONS AS A REFLECTIVE TIME

In Sanctuary, we often curated services using stations – different areas/zones where people could go and explore, try, do, think, engage and participate. The key to all our services was active participation. This was not unusual in the world of alternative worship groups in the 1990s and 2000s; the term alternative worship has now mostly been replaced by pioneer, or fresh expression. We found that this way of curating a service enabled different ages to participate and engage. As the children in the group got older, we often encouraged them to take part in planning and designing the services. One Lent, we decided to use the Examen. We used a list of questions based on an interpretation of the Examen by John O'Donohue (2008). We all used the Examen questions over the Lent period and then for our Easter service we each took one from the list and created a station for this. During the service we explored and engaged with each of the stations. At the time, our children also took one question each; they were aged 9 and 11. Examples of the stations they created are below. In Chapter 10 you can find a list of the questions and some of the stations we made.

Where did I allow myself to receive love? By Lily Mainstone-Cotton

The following words were written alongside the shape of a body drawn on large paper:

Have you ever hidden yourself away?

Ever just wanted a hug and to be told you're loved?

Write down on the heart sticky notes where you have received love.

This could be a place or a person.

How did it make you feel?

Once you have done it stick the notes on the body.

What dreams did I create last night? By Summer Mainstone-Cotton

These words were written on paper inside a pop-up tent, with pillows and a blanket.

Paper

It can be a real life dream that you want to come true or it can be a dream you had in your head. Whatever it is draw or write it on the paper.

Tent

Relax and rest whilst you ponder on your dreams and aspirations or the types of dreams you had tucked up in bed.
Are they good or bad?
Do they mean anything?
Is God communicating with you through your head?
Or are they just pure nonsense?

The same year, we took this idea to Greenbelt and set it up as an installation for people to explore during the festival. We found that each station encouraged people to stop, be still, listen, pray, reflect. The installation was in the venue where we ran 'Messy Space', a family play and worship space. This wasn't a quiet space, but these stations introduced spaces within the larger space for all ages to take a moment and stop, to find some quietness. As we know, quietness and stillness do not have to be about the environment we are in, but are also about finding space and quietness within ourselves. The tent station created by Summer was particularly popular; many people of all ages took themselves into the tent for a moment of space and finding some quiet within themselves. I believe using this style of worship helped our children to find quietness within themselves and supported others to do this. We found over the course of the weekend that many hundreds of people stopped at the stations and spent time in finding a moment of stillness within a busy festival.

This included children of many different ages. At the end of the book, I share some further examples of a few of the stations we created for the Examen.

INTERVIEW WITH WILL AND ESTHER ABOUT THEIR EXPERIENCE OF USING STILLNESS AND MINDFULNESS WITH CHILDREN

In this interview I am speaking with Will and Esther Taylor. Will is a child counsellor and the pair have run children's work in churches for many years.

CAN YOU TELL ME ABOUT YOUR EXPERIENCE OF USING CONTEMPLATIVE AND STILLNESS PRACTICE WITH CHILDREN IN CHURCH?

W: We always have a prayer tent, a cheap tent that we put up in the room. It has cushions in and the flaps are rolled back so we can see. We tell the children that they can go in at any point; for example, if we are doing children songs and they want some time out, or if we are having a story. If they need time out, they can go into the tent and then come back and re-engage when they are ready. What is really important is that the children know that they have our full permission to step out at any point to have space for themselves in the tent. The programme comes second to the child's needs in this way and we ensure that they know that.

At the end of our children sessions we put 10 to 15 minutes aside to have some quiet time, put on ambient music, without words, get the children to spread around the room, lie down, eyes closed and have stillness. The question we give them to consider is 'What has God said to you today?' We use this with children aged 5 to 11 and young leaders.

HOW LONG WOULD YOU DO THIS STILLNESS PRACTICE FOR?
E: About 5 minutes. At the end, we ask if anyone has anything they want to share. Children can say things if they want to.

W: It's about giving space; often children don't have space to just consider, just to be. Before they rush back into the business of post-church, biscuits, cakes, drinks, going home, we give them space to be quiet and think.

FROM YOUR EXPERIENCE OF HOW STRESSED CHILDREN ARE TODAY, YOU MUST HAVE SEEN A RANGE OF CHILDREN'S WELLBEING IN YOUR GROUP. THINKING ABOUT THE QUIET TIME YOU CREATE, WHAT IS ITS BENEFIT?
W: We have quite a few children who are adopted and fostered, and they can find life hard and be a bit more chaotic. Other children experience the craziness of life. We have wanted to say your time and relationship with God is yours and not mine to give you, and you need to listen to what your relationship with God is; you need to give yourself time to think about who you really are and you may get a revelation on this. You won't get it if I just tell you what I think about myself and you won't get it if we just do loud crazy games and songs. Connecting with something a bit deeper spiritually is really important. In that quiet place, understand the still, small, quiet voice that is God, but also learn to hear what your own voice is like. Children don't know what that inner voice is; lots of adults don't know what their inner voice is like. There is always noise where you can receive affirmation externally but you don't often stop and listen to your own voice telling you that, so when you do hear the inner voice, it is often the critical voice.

E: We have done prayer stations in the past. Within the church context we often underestimate how children can connect with God, on a spiritual level, giving them that space, facilitating those things. We have set up stations offering different activities with instructions. We had one with an outline of a body and sticking plasters and asked children to write names of people that were ill, or to write things that were worrying them, and they stuck the plasters on the body. We had seven or eight different stations, with a young leader at each station; the children just went and explored and participated.

W: Once with our older group, the youth group, we gave them the resource cupboard and told them to express something about God, and we let them make what they wanted. They were creating prayer spaces for everyone else to use and explore. They had some amazing ideas. Two girls got a UV light and UV pens – theirs was about God shining light into the places we can't see – and they wrote stuff, and it was only when the light shone on it that you could see the writing. So often there is not a belief that children can connect at that depth with their faith. What we have always wanted to do is give space for children to experience the opportunity of connecting with something on a much deeper level, and testing that and trusting them.

MY REFLECTIONS ON WILL AND ESTHER'S EXPERIENCE

I love the way Will and Esther have found ways to support children and young people to be curious and ask questions.

So often as adults we can find this a challenge. I also agree with Esther's view that we can underestimate how children can connect with God. As adults we tend to constrain the way children can connect with God because of our own limitations. We forget how curious, questioning and creative children and young people are. I believe that if we open up our own thinking in how we support, model and scaffold children's learning, then we are enabling children to learn much more.

REFERENCES
Draper, B. (2017) *Soulfulness Deepening the Mindful Life*. London: Hodder and Stoughton.

Keating, N. (2017) *Meditation with Children: A Resource for Teachers and Parents*. Dublin: Veritas.

Mainstone-Cotton, S. (2017a) *Promoting Young Children's Emotional Health and Wellbeing*. London: Jessica Kingsley Publishers.

Mainstone-Cotton, S. (2017b) *Promoting Emotional Wellbeing in Early Years Staff*. London: Jessica Kingsley Publishers.

Miyazaki, Y. (2012) Nature therapy Ted Talk. Accessed on 14/01/2019 at www.youtube.com/watch?v=MD4rlWqp7Po&list=SP629FCC64F4B98ED5&index=27

O'Donohue, J. (2008) *To Bless the Space between Us: A Book of Blessings*. New York: Convergent Books.

Stead, T. (2016) *Mindfulness and Christian Spirituality*. London: SPCK.

Williams, F. (2017) *The Nature Fix: Why Nature Makes Us Happier, Healthier and More Creative*. London: W.W. Norton & Company.

Williams, M. and Penman, D. (2011) *Mindfulness: A Practical Guide to Finding Peace in a Frantic World*. London: Little Brown Book Group.

CHAPTER 3

CONTEMPLATIVE PRACTICE AS PART OF THE CHRISTIAN TRADITION

As I have mentioned in previous chapters, mindfulness and stillness practice is viewed with caution by some in the church, fearing that it has links to Eastern religions. I have heard many concerns that it is linked with Buddhism and for this reason we should not engage in it. Others have told me that by engaging in a meditative practice, we are opening ourselves to dark forces. This chapter will look at how stillness and contemplative, mindful, meditative practice has been part of the Christian tradition for a very long time. Benignus O'Rourke (2011) believes that for the last 600 years the gift of using silent prayer, which used to be a rich part of Christian tradition, has almost been abandoned and completely forgotten. O'Rourke suggests that a Benedictine monk called John Main (1926–1982) was one of the first people in modern times to remind us in the West of this almost lost tradition. This came about at a time when many were going to the East to find a different religious experience. John Main was working in India and discovered the Eastern form of silent meditation, He looked back at his own tradition to find a long history of silence, meditation and prayer that he felt had been forgotten. When John Main came back to the UK he worked hard to get the practice of Christian meditation embedded in practice there. He recommended using a prayer word, Maranatha, and to repeat this as four syllables of equal length: Ma-ra-na-tha. There is a website dedicated to him where you can listen to his insight and words.[1] He suggested that Christians can often find the notion of using a mantra a frightening idea for prayer and some suggest it is non-Christian. He feels that it is sad that we have lost the long tradition of this type of prayer and suggests we should be listening to God; not bringing lots of words, but sitting and listening. He proposes that before we can pray, we need to become still and only then can we be aware of the loving spirit of Jesus. He recognises that many Christians think this is only for saints and monks, but he argues that this is for all of us.

As part of this chapter I have interviewed four people who use contemplative practice as a daily part of their lives. These are an Orthodox nun from the Russian Orthodox Church, a monk from Downside Abbey and a Vicar and Chaplain, Ian and Gail Adams. The aim of these interviews is to hear directly from people who have long used this practice and looked closely at the long history behind it. The chapter will conclude with some recommended further reading. In this chapter I am not claiming to be a theologian or an academic, but I will first briefly highlight and link to old traditions that I think we can learn much from today.

---

[1]   www.johnmain.org

JESUS FINDING SOLITUDE

There are many examples throughout the gospels of how Jesus sought out solitude and silence. There were many times when Jesus actively chose to be away from people, to spend time with his Father, and just be, to be still and pray. Some examples of these are as follows:

> At once the spirit sent him out into the wilderness, and he was in the wilderness for forty days, being tempted by Satan. He was with the wild animals, and angels attended him. (Mark 1:12)

> Very early in the morning, while it was still dark, Jesus got up, left the house and went off to a solitary place, where he prayed. (Mark 1:35)

> When Jesus heard what had happened (John the Baptist beheading) he withdrew privately to a solitary place. (Matthew 14:13)

> Jesus went out to a mountainside to pray, and spent the night praying to God. (Luke 6:12)

MONASTIC RHYTHMS

We often think of silent, contemplative practice in the form of a monastic tradition. There is a growing interest in monasticism; in 2005 there was a BBC TV programme called *The Monastery*, following five men who joined a Benedictine monastic community at Worth Abbey for 40 days and nights. The five men were asked to take part in the community life, to experience silence and take part in the rhythm of monastic life, which included meeting six times a day to pray. The monks at Worth monastery felt that the ancient monastic tradition had something to offer our modern, busy and full lives. The men were asked to spend the 40 days listening to themselves, to others and to God. Over three programmes, the viewer was invited to observe how the men, who were all from very different backgrounds – some with faith some unsure – managed in the 40 days. What was clear by the end was that all five men had been moved by their 40 days' encounter. Eighteen months later, the men were invited back for a weekend. All five men were still using the meditation and silence practices as they all recognised they really benefited them.

As a follow-on from the programme the Abbot, Christopher Jamison wrote a book about how to find sanctuary in everyday life (2006). He refers to the many people who attend Worth Abbey for a retreat and to find sanctuary and how often they say their lives are too busy and they don't know how to halt this. Abbot Jamison suggests that we choose to be busy; this is a life choice we make and we can change this. He suggests that this is partly linked with our consumerist society urging us to constantly work harder in order to buy more. I think it is very easy to feel that we have to be busy; it often links into our feelings of self-worth. However, I also recognise there are times and seasons when life is very busy; I remember when our children were small and we both shared the child care and both worked part-time, it was and felt very busy. It was hard to find time to stop. I know parents who are holding down several jobs in a desperate attempt to get enough money to live on. At these times, the challenge can be finding a rhythm that works, but if we can find a regular time in the day to stop, find silence, be with God, this is very beneficial. The times that work will of course be different for everyone. I am an early morning person; I love early mornings and I swim at 6.30 a.m. every day. If I try to stop and find silence at the end of the day, I promptly fall asleep, whereas early morning works perfectly for me.

CRAVING SILENCE

Abbot Christopher Jamison describes how many of the people who attend retreats at the Abbey say they do this as they crave the silence it will bring: the silence in the building and the surroundings. However, in practice many people find the silence very challenging and experience their minds as full and loud and not at all silent. Jamison reminds us that sitting with silence and learning how to find silence takes a lot of practice. Martin Laird (2006) writes about how silence is the homeland to which Christian pilgrims are being repeatedly called but recognises this is not always easy. In the Bible we can see how being in silence can be tough: 'So I remained utterly silent, not even saying anything good. But my anguish increased: my heart grew hot within me. While I meditated, the fire burned' (Psalm 39: 2–3). And yet throughout the Bible we are reminded time and again that God is in the silence. God showed himself to Elijah; Elijah was told to stand on a mountain:

> Then a great and powerful wind tore the mountains apart and shattered the rocks before the Lord, but the Lord was not in the wind. After the wind there was an earthquake, but the Lord was not in the earthquake.

After the earthquake came a fire, but the Lord was not in the fire. And after the fire came a gentle whisper (1 Kings 19:12)

On many occasions in the Bible we are called to be silent and still: 'When you are on your beds search your heart and be silent' (Psalm 4).

FOLLOWING THE MONASTIC WAYS
There is still a growing interest in the monastic ways. There are a few groups that follow the idea of monasticism and are trying to figure out how it works for communities now; some groups refer to this as new monasticism. The Archbishop of Canterbury has set up a community called St Anselm[2], for adults aged 20 to 35, which offers people the chance to be part of a community sharing their lives, service, prayer and study. There are other groups who are not choosing to live as part of a community but want to learn how to embed some of the features of monastic life; for example, regular silence practice, a pattern for prayer. Moot[3], in London, and the Northumbria Community[4] are two examples of new monastic groups.

Since the TV programme, *The Monastery,* there have been other programmes following a similar storyline and more recently there have also been programmes focusing on slowing down and observing and encountering stillness. In 2017 there was a series of programmes on BBC4 called

---

[2] http://stanselm.org.uk
[3] www.moot.uk.net
[4] www.northumbriacommunity.org/who-we-are/introducing-the-community/a-new-monasticism

Retreat: Meditations from a Monastery[5] describing 'going in search of inner peace in three monasteries in Britain'. These documentaries followed life in the monastery, with clips of the monks making bread, winding up a clock, sitting to pray and so on, and each programme lasted one hour. There was minimal conversation. In many ways this was quite strange TV, but it was also curiously soothing and calming. My sense is that these programmes are being made because there is a recognition that things in our society are not right; that our lifestyles are not conducive to wellbeing. A section of society is looking to the monastic traditions to see what it can learn.

One of the monasteries filmed was at Downside in Somerset, close to where I live. An interview with Father Christopher from Downside, talking about his experience of practising silence and contemplative prayer, follows.

INTERVIEW WITH FATHER CHRISTOPHER

WHY DO YOU THINK THAT STILLNESS, THE PRACTICE OF SILENT PRAYER, IS IMPORTANT FOR US TODAY, IN THIS WORLD, AT THIS TIME?

Mental prayer, silent prayer, can be seen as the least obvious. Some people think it is only for monks and nuns, but actually it is very important for everybody, because silent prayer is putting yourself in the presence of God. That is hard, as there are no words and it is hard because you cannot switch the mind off. People always complain, 'Oh, I am distracted as soon as I sit down to pray'; that's okay,

---

[5]   www.bbc.co.uk/programmes/b09c0hwb

that is the way it is. The silent prayer techniques which are very age old, they have been substantiated by our modern experience and reinforced by our modern experience, because life is so crowded and we are so assailed by our thoughts and communication and noise that it becomes even more crucial. I think God is leading one into deeper waters, like in the story when they are on the boat fishing and Jesus said cast your net on the other side. I think God is telling us, when we have all the distraction and things, to give up fishing on the one side and come to the other side. I think the other side is silent prayer. So you can't switch the mind off, but what you can do is use the mantra. The mantra is a way of putting aside the crowding of thoughts; you can't get rid of them but you can lessen their effect on you. One of the images I like to use is the black plastic that you put down to put weeds out; you only let the plants go through the holes you put in. The mantra is like that, it blankets out the other things.

WHAT DO YOU MEAN BY THE MANTRA?

The mantra is a word or phrase that you repeat. A phrase often used is an Aramaic word 'Maranatha': this is the word for 'Come Lord Jesus', it has a beat to it. As far as technique is concerned, it fits on the breath. You repeat that. That deals with the active mind and lets you stand back a bit.

THERE ARE CONCERNS AROUND HOW SILENT, MEDITATIVE PRACTICE IS LINKED TO EASTERN RELIGIONS AND CONCERN AROUND THE DARKNESS WE MAYBE OPENING OURSELVES TO. HOW WOULD YOU RESPOND TO THAT?

God is the God of the East as well as the West; he has chosen to be born among us in the West as man, but he could have chosen to be born elsewhere. Meanwhile, he may have revealed himself in different ways to different people. For instance, they have a conscience in the East as well as in the West, which is God's voice in their hearts; and he may have revealed himself to them in their ways of praying, so if it fits we can wear the same shoes. This argument can be used for prayer, but that doesn't mean it should apply to everything else.

You can take the good and leave out the bad. There is a man called John Main, who I knew; he was a monk somewhere else. He was in the Irish foreign diplomatic service, in the Far East and while there he learnt about Eastern meditation practices and applied them. He brought them back to the UK and tried hard to promote this in his monastery. When I knew him, it was about 1960. He worked hard to promote this more widely. One of his collaborators is a monk and he now runs the world community for Christian meditation in the UK,[6] so it has continued.

HEARING FROM DIFFERENT TRADITIONS

For this chapter of the book, I wanted to be able hear from people who have a deep knowledge and understanding of the ancient practice of stillness and contemplative practice, but I was also keen to hear from people who are coming from different Christian traditions. It's easy to become familiar with our own strand of church practice and never hear from others. In the city I live in, Bath, there is a Russian Orthodox community and part of that community is a woman called

---

[6]   www.christianmeditation.org.uk

Mother Sarah. She is an Orthodox nun who lives in the city and works as a chaplain at the university and hospital. Below is my conversation with Mother Sarah about her experience.

INTERVIEW WITH MOTHER SARAH

WHY DO YOU THINK THAT STILLNESS, THE PRACTICE OF SILENT PRAYER, IS IMPORTANT FOR US TODAY, IN THIS WORLD, AT THIS TIME?

I think it's really important because people so easily lose touch with their centre and the centre of what gives them strength; they easily lose touch with God. People need times and opportunities when they can reconnect with God and reconnect with the sources of their own strength, which comes to the same thing. But we are surrounded by so many distractions: media, technology distractions, stress of life, the exhaustion of life; people need time to regroup inwardly and get back in touch with God. It restores us. People are more than just mind and body, they are soul and spirit as well and the human system needs time to bring itself back together and recentre itself and reintegrate itself, and those times of stillness and silence and contemplative prayer bring the whole person back together again from all the dissipation that occurs in daily living.

THERE ARE CONCERNS AROUND HOW SILENT, MEDITATIVE PRACTICE IS LINKED TO EASTERN RELIGIONS AND CONCERN AROUND THE DARKNESS WE MAYBE OPENING OURSELVES TO. HOW WOULD YOU RESPOND TO THAT?

I think you can answer that in two ways. One is to say that if you look at the Christian tradition where it is strong, you can absolutely demonstrate that it has been there from the beginning. People who are doing it now are aware that they're entering into an ancient practice; the Lord himself went into the desert on his own in silence. It just doesn't stand up to examination saying it hasn't always been part of the Christian tradition. The other answer is, well what are you actually doing? Are you focusing on the Lord Jesus Christ? If you're not then it's not Christian. It is my personal belief that mindfulness where you teach someone to still, using breathing or watching thoughts or whatever you choose, if you are restoring integrity to a human being you are in fact bringing them back to God, because God is the foundation of all life. Even if the person can't put a name to God, once they become more whole they are on their way back to God. It all depends on whether you have a very dualistic attitude, with God there and then the wicked world over there, or whether you see God as actually undergirding everything and particularly human wholeness and wellbeing.

SOME FIND STILLNESS PRACTICE REALLY DIFFICULT, DO YOU HAVE ANY TIPS?

Don't be rigid about how it has to be; be willing to experiment. You don't have to be rigidly tied to a method, it is fluid. Walking meditation is widely recommended but the simple answer is that you don't need to feel it has to fit into a mould. Perhaps try doing it with other people, maybe belonging to a group that meets once a week, as this can give you a routine and bring you back to the group. The social support of others who are doing the same thing is important.

DO YOU HAVE ANY EXPERIENCE OF USING THESE PRACTICES WITH CHILDREN?

Yes and no; I haven't ever tried to do the Jesus Prayer, which is the way most common in the Orthodox Church, with small children. For most of us in our services, there is a big communal effort to incorporate the children into the worship, so there is a stillness in having to be in one place and not be standing up and sitting down and getting the hymn book out; our worship does induce a certain level of stillness, because you are in one place and you're not moving. You definitely calm down and the children have to learn to do that. Initially they are in parents' arms and taken out when restless and then they are sitting on the floor and they are taken out when they get restless; but it's a huge judgement call for the parents, deciding when they are going to take them out. It's a real challenge of support and understanding from the congregation who are getting irritated at the restless child, but they totally understand the parents wants to be in church as well. It's a big community challenge, but overall, when it works well, the children learn to be still for an extended period and I think we give them something invaluable. It's not just the fact they are not rushing around, but it's the fact they learn to be attentive to something beyond the external distractions.

REFLECTIONS FROM THESE INTERVIEWS

What stood out for me in the interview with Mother Sarah is the deep understanding of how contemplative and stillness practice can underpin and support good mental wellbeing. Mother Sarah was hugely aware of the stresses of our society today, and could see the toxic nature of how so many of us live. I particularly loved the way she described how mindfulness can help to restore integrity to a human being, and through this you are bringing them back to God. With both Father Christopher and Mother Sarah, I found it helpful to hear their acknowledgement that practising contemplative and silent practice can be challenging and it is not always easy. I particularly liked Father Christopher's suggestion of using a mantra and the word 'Maranatha' that he suggested. This was a new word to me; I had read about it as part of my research for the book and first became aware of it through Noel Keating's book (2017); it is the word he uses with children in meditation. Since the interview with Father Christopher I have started to use this word while swimming. I have found it really helpful.

WHAT WE CAN LEARN FROM MONASTICISM

It can be easy to look at the life of nuns and monks and feel that they are very distant from our own lives. However I feel there are things we can learn from them, one of the main ones being that having a pattern and rhythm to our lives is beneficial. Many in monastic orders have the daily routine of stopping to pray several times in a day – to have times of silence. I noticed on *The Monastery* TV programme that during their time of silence, several monks would choose to sit outside, looking over the garden or a field; they all seemed to have their spot that they went to. Finding a rhythm and pattern for our own lives can be difficult, particularly if you are a parent of young children or busy working and so on. However, intentionally putting in place our own rhythms can really help to enhance our wellbeing and relationship with God. Seven years ago I started swimming each Monday to Friday morning. This came about partly to get fit, but also out of a recognition that I needed a time in the day when I could be outside of the family and work routine, to pray and spend time with God. Swimming may not sound like the most natural place to find inner stillness and silence; however, it works really well for me. My swimming has become a prayerful, meditative time. Over the years of swimming, I have moved through praying a lot with words during my swimming, to now mostly using the Jesus Prayer or no words, but the repetitive act of swimming strokes up and down the pool is very meditative. The other space I regularly go to, to be with God and experience silence, is the community meadow behind our house. During the summer months I often walk barefoot around the meadow. The act of barefoot walking forces to me to slow down, to notice, to bring stillness within. Because I have returned to the meadow many, many times to pray, this space has become a prayerful space for me. This is the space where I have walked and cried over the health of my parents and cried out to God over the despair of losing my job. This is the space I go to when I am emotionally worn down from the challenges of working with traumatised 4-year-olds. This is my go-to silent space.

Questions for reflection

- What patterns, rhythms do you have in your life for prayer, stopping and finding silence? Is there anything about these patterns that you need to refine/change?

- How comfortable are you with silence? If this leaves you feeling uncomfortable, do you know why?
- Do you have a space or a place you can go to, where you can just be, where you can encounter stillness and be with God?

A practice to try

If you are new to trying out silence practice, if you are someone who would usually rather fill the space with words or music, try this for a moment.

Find a place where you are comfortable to sit. Turn off devices around you if you can.

Close your eyes or lower your gaze.

Place your hand on your tummy and notice your breathing; notice the breath as you breathe in and breathe out.

If it helps, you could say a word in your head as you breathe in and out. Words I often use are 'Be Still' or try the word 'Ma-ra-na-tha'.

Try saying the word 'Be' as you breathe in and the word 'Still' as you breathe out, or:

Ma – breathe in
Ra – breathe out
Na – breathe in
Tha – breathe out

Use this for around 10 or 12 breaths and then open your eyes.

You may have found your mind was busy while you did this, with thoughts floating in. That's okay, that is what minds do. The important thing is you started. Some say that with practice it gets easier; I am not sure about that. On some days my mind can be quieter; other days it is full. But I have learnt that is okay. The important element is stopping and intentionally being in a place of silence, to be with God.

DESERT FATHERS AND MOTHERS

Many of us in the church may have a vague knowledge about the Desert Fathers and Mothers; we may have heard the name but not be aware of their significance. When people say to me that meditation practice is unsafe and I mention the Desert Fathers and Mothers, I am often met with a shrug or a look of uncertainty. I am going to briefly explain who they were and their significance. If you are already familiar with this, you may want to skip this small section.

In the third, fourth and fifth centuries a group of men and women chose to live in the deserts, mainly in Syria, Palestine and Egypt. They chose to live a life of celibacy, solitude, fasting, silence, prayer and poverty. They have become known as the Desert Fathers and Mothers. They mostly lived as hermits or sometimes they would have people living near them who learnt from them. They spent their time meditating on the Bible – which they committed to memory – praying, being in silence and doing repetitive manual work such as rope making. They lived and worked in small spaces, sometimes a cave or a hut. Living in the natural world was a very important element of their lifestyle. For them, it was the place where they encountered the presence of God (Ward 2003). These early Desert Fathers and Mothers have influenced monasteries and convents today, but also many others who are re-engaging with contemplative traditions. Looking back at how these men and women lived their lives, there is much that we can learn from them. One story I particularly like from this time is of a group of people asking a Desert Father named Macarius about how they should pray. His answer to them was they didn't need to use many words;

instead they could say to God 'Lord have mercy on me, as you will and as you know', or if they were in conflict they could say 'Lord help me' (Ward 2003, p.132). There are some who view the Desert Fathers and Mothers as escapists fleeing the world. The same is sometimes also said of monastic orders today; however the Desert Fathers and Mothers often had people visiting them, to gain wisdom and learn from them; it could be said they were equipping the wider church. In the same way, monastic orders today are a place where others are able to go, learn from, seek wisdom and find support. This was really clear from the TV programme, *The Monastery*.

THE IMPACT THE DESERT FATHERS AND MOTHERS HAVE HAD

Over the years, the teaching of the Desert Fathers and Mothers has influenced many people. Augustine Hippo, who was around in 390 AD and has influenced both the Catholic and Protestant Church, firmly believed we needed to come back to knowing that God is within us and speaks to us within the silence of our hearts (O'Rourke 2011). In our prayer life it is so easy to get caught up in our words, in praying for things that are our own agenda, and we often teach this way of praying to children from a young age. Looking back, you will probably find this is also how you were taught to have a relationship with God – to list all the things on your mind. Thomas Merton (2005) suggests that it can be risky to pray and there is a danger of our prayer words getting between God and us. He suggests that we cut out words; that we let Jesus pray through us, which is really what Augustine was saying in 390 AD.

WRITING TODAY ON CONTEMPLATIVE STILLNESS PRACTICE

There are a growing number of books which explain, unpick and guide us through Christian contemplative practice today. If you are new to reading on this subject, Ian Adams' *Cave Refectory Road: Monastic Rhythms for Contemporary Living* (2010) is an excellent place to start your reading. This book introduces you to the monastic tradition and how it can be beneficial to us today. Theologians such as Martin Laird, Richard Rohr, Thomas Merton and Ian Adams have studied and practised contemplative practice for many years and are able to offer excellent insight and guidance. Martin Laird (2006) suggests there are two contemplative practices which are the foundations of the Christian tradition: stillness and awareness. His book suggests ways we can re-engage with these practices. Richard Rohr set up the Centre for action and Contemplation.[7] The Centre's website offers courses, reflections, meditations and contemplations. The vision behind this set-up was that action and contemplation could not be two separate ideas: contemplation needed to underpin action. From my own experience, this makes so much sense; I firmly believe my own work as a nurture consultant with 4-year-olds who find life very hard is only possible because of the underpinning of my contemplative practice. I need to be in a calm, emotionally stable place to be a safe person for these children; daily contemplative practice helps me to do that.

Richard Rohr talks about how the goal of prayer is to give us access to God and enables us to listen to God. He also

---

[7]   https://cac.org

suggests that prayer is about enabling us to experience the indwelling presence of God. He argues that if we over-think during prayer we are unable to access God, as what we already think and agree with gets in the way. Rohr proposes that God is unfamiliar and mysterious and we need to be open to this. He acknowledges this can be very hard for many adults. However, I think this is where children have such openness and an ability to really engage with God. Young children are naturally curious, interested and inquisitive. Young children are engaged in the awe and wonder around us. I would suggest that building on this natural fascination and curiosity with young children supports us in introducing them to stillness practice. The end section of the book will have many practical suggestions on how to do this.

My final interview for this chapter is with Gail and Ian Adams. Ian is an ordained Anglican priest, a writer and a poet. Gail is spiritual mentor, and is currently working as a chaplain at Ridley Hall. Both Ian and Gail run 'beloved life',[8] a website and space for spiritual direction and prac-tices. They also deliver retreats.

INTERVIEW WITH GAIL AND IAN

WHY DO YOU THINK THAT STILLNESS, THE PRACTICE OF SILENT PRAYER, IS IMPORTANT FOR US TODAY, IN THIS WORLD, AT THIS TIME?

I: We need to find our place of belonging, a place from which we can navigate the world, which pushes and pulls us

---

8   www.belovedlife.org/about

in all directions. I have a commitment to stillness; it locates me, locates me in a place of belonging that feels precious and good. A place in which I am loved and all is okay.

G: It feels like coming home, a place where I can be me and God can be God. From this place of peaceful centredness I am better equipped to deal with the stuff of life, I carry it with me.

WHY IS THAT DIFFERENT TO LOTS OF WORDS OR A NOISE SERVICE? IS IT DIFFERENT, AND IF SO HOW?

G: For me it's different as I feel sometimes words get in the way. I try to let go of words in order to be more present to God. Letting go is part of the coming home. This realignment into presence is a practice I try to do in daily rituals like putting on the kettle!

I: Words matter to me; I write words, perform words. There is also something rich about letting go of words, getting to the end of my words. It's a bit scary too. It's a commitment to reality, recognising that words can get in the way of reality. What if I just shut up? What if it is just my breathing? Wow, that really matters now, if all I have is that side of breathing. My personal sense is it's a good thing; there is a belonging, a hopefulness in that.

G: When I can let go of words in my stillness practice I find it's a place where truth lives, where all the negative voices about me are quietened. A place where I come back to who I really am, hidden in Christ.

THERE ARE CONCERNS AROUND HOW SILENT, MEDITATIVE PRACTICE IS LINKED TO EASTERN RELIGIONS AND CONCERN AROUND THE DARKNESS WE MAYBE OPENING OURSELVES TO. HOW WOULD YOU RESPOND TO THAT?

I: I sense that the contemplative path has always been part of the Christian tradition, a golden thread, but we have often lost it. It's been submerged in our desire for easy answers or for power. But it's always been there, nurtured particularly by the monastics in their commitment to prayer and to stillness. It needs to be recovered. There is only true reality; if something is true it is true, whatever you call it, so let's commit ourselves to truth. If you look, Jesus models for us the contemplative path; he models how to do it, practically going to the quiet place, the hills. His teachings are very contemplative; the Beatitudes and what they are pointing to, they are contemplative.

LOTS OF PEOPLE SAY THEY FIND SILENCE HARD. I THINK A LOT OF PEOPLE ARE SCARED BY THIS. FOR THOSE WHO ARE TRYING BUT FIND IT HARD, DO YOU HAVE ANY WISDOM ON THAT?

G: We always say that stillness is awkward, and it is, it's a practice. All practices take practise. Silence is hard to find these days but we carry stillness within us; it is waiting to be found.

I: It becomes more familiar, like putting a shirt or a coat on. Put something new on and it feels weird, but as you put on a much-loved garment it begins to mould around you and feel more comfortable.

G: I sense that part of what makes the practice hard is the onslaught of our thoughts when we go into stillness. Finding a way to let go of these thoughts by focusing instead on our breath or a prayer word helps. The head fizzing with thoughts is normal. It's been said that every thought is an opportunity to let go and come back to the God who is always present to us.

I: The awkwardness is important and natural; because of the layers of stuff we protect ourselves with, it's important we go there. Its natural, it's fine; it doesn't mean it's not working, but it's helpful to find a practice that enables us to handle that, to recognise the thoughts and then lay them aside in some way. There are various practices to do that. Increasingly to be open, to be present, just fleetingly. Some people find sitting in silence natural and that it feels good; for many of us that is much more difficult. We can find that stillness within movement as well. For me, my running is an important part of my stillness prayer practice, literally running out of words, as I can't say any words, as I am just trying to breathe with the running, but also letting go of my internal dialogue as I run, giving myself to the running, to being present – and rediscovering in the process that I belong, that I love and am loved, and that 'all shall be well'.

REFECTION ON THIS CONVERSATION

I love Ian's description of contemplative practice being like a 'golden thread' in the Christian tradition, but one that we have lost. I also love how both Ian and Gail refer to contemplative practice as a feeling of coming home. That has been my experience; I rarely experience God in the noise of a loud service or band-led worship. I most often experience God when I am outside, swimming in the open sea, in the still places and the beauty of creation. I also echo their comments around the fact that this is a practice, and it does not necessarily get easier. In fact as I am writing the bulk of this book, I am doing it during the school summer holidays, when I have a break from working in schools. Each morning I swim and then I write, and I weave in time for stillness practice. However, I am finding that hard, whilst writing this book, reading and researching, thinking deeply about this practice, the practice I am finding tricky. There are some days when it does not come naturally at all, but I have learnt that is okay.

MAKING SPACE

As Iain and Gail mention in their interviews and Martin Laird (2011) talks about in his second book, being in silence as part of a regular practice takes practise. Martin Laird (2011) suggests that the more we do it, the harder it can become; this is not about finding an easy practice. As I mentioned before one key to this practice is finding a time and space that works for you. This can be about physical space as well as time space within the day. The Orthodox Church use Icons a lot within their prayer. I have friends who have created prayer spaces within their house; some have Icons as part of this. You could also have a candle, a holding cross, prayer beads, a cushion or prayer stool. I have a friend who was a curate's wife. She made her own prayer space in the cupboard under the stairs. At the time they had a young family of four children and time to herself was rare, but by having the space under the stairs she was able to find moments to take herself away and be still, be with God. If you make a prayer space in your house, your children will see and learn the importance of finding space and quiet to be with God. You may also find your children start to use it too.

PRACTICES THAT CAN SUPPORT CONTEMPLATIVE STILLNESS TIME

As I have said earlier the book, I do believe it is only possible to teach and support children in meditation, stillness and contemplation if you regularly do this yourself. If this is new to you, I would suggest you start to find ways to practise this in your own life. Below are a few suggestions on how you could get started. For further practise, Ian Adams' second book, *Running over Rocks* (2013), has 52 practices for you try. Also Tim Stead's second book, *See, Love, Be: Mindfulness and the Spiritual Life* (2018), has an 8-week mindfulness programme you can use. The book includes a CD, with meditations to use too.

Exercise 1: Sitting in silence, praying without words

Find a space to sit in silence, without distractions. You may like to have an Icon, a holding cross or a pebble. You should be comfortable, with your back straight and feet on the ground. Set a timer for five minutes; I use an app called 'insight timer' on my iPad.

Sit in the silence; holding a cross or pebble or looking at an Icon can sometimes help to give you something to bring your attention back to if your mind wanders.

Focusing on your breathing can help.

Come to this time without using words, just sit and be with God.

The more you do this, slowly increase the time you set aside.

Exercise 2: The Jesus Prayer

If you are finding the move to prayer without words just too hard, you could try the Jesus Prayer. This prayer has come out of the Orthodox tradition. A short, useful introduction to this prayer and how to use it is the book by Simon Barrington-Ward (1996). Using the Jesus Prayer links us into many before us and those with us also using this prayer. The words to use are:

Lord Jesus Christ, Son of God, have mercy on me.

Pause and repeat and continue to repeat these words.

Some add to this: have mercy on me a sinner or have mercy on... and name a person.

This prayer also works well with movement. I often use this prayer when I am swimming, particularly if someone is on my mind and concerning me.

Swim stroke one – Lord Jesus Christ
Swim stroke two – Son of God
Swim stroke three – have mercy on...

and repeat and repeat.

I want to end this chapter by hearing from someone who uses contemplative practice and is from a more evangelical part of the church, as I am aware that the other interviews have been from other parts of the church family. Flic is a joint leader with her husband at the Vineyard church in Bath. Flic is fairly new to contemplative practice.

INTERVIEW WITH FLIC NEWPORT

HOW DID YOU FIND OUT ABOUT CONTEMPLATIVE PRACTICE?
I am training to be a spiritual director. The training is five weekend retreats a year. They use a lot of contemplative practice and I am reading set texts around that.

UNTIL YOU STARTED THE COURSE, WERE YOU FAMILIAR WITH CONTEMPLATIVE PRACTICE?

Not really; I had heard of the Northumberland community and last year I heard of a daily reading book and at the start and end of this there was a two-minute silent practice, so I knew a little.

DO YOU USE CONTEMPLATIVE PRACTICE REGULARLY AND IF SO WHY?

Currently I like to use it daily as a 10-minute practice at the start of the day. As a discipline on the course, they set up a practice each month to try different things. One of those is centring prayer, starting by taking a 2-minute silence and learning to meet with God in that way. Initially that was a real struggle and I came to recognise that in this time of information overload and social media, phones and the Internet, my mind is on fast track all the time. I found 2 minutes of silence initially was hard. Then using centring prayer to sit with God without words, just to sit with God, enjoy his presence and recognise he is enjoying yours, you don't need to say anything. Through this practice, I totally fell in love with it as a way of meeting with God. Not that every time I feel like it is fireworks and roses, but I really did meet with him and was blown away by that. This is really rich and I would love more people to know about it. Not everyone is going to be into contemplative practice, but in this day and age, it is such a skill.

YOU ARE LEADING A CHURCH AND YOU USE CONTEMPLATIVE PRACTICE IN YOUR OWN EVERYDAY PRACTICE: ARE YOU ABLE TO BRING THAT INTO CHURCH?

I love to incorporate it where I can in our services. At the moment it doesn't look formalised; we will do a chunk of sung worship in the morning and then we will have some space where people can share prophetic words. After that I will allow silence, giving space for those words to be thought about, or then we will do a talk and we will do a time of ministry and we try to have some space for silence, but we are talking minutes. I recognise that for some people, the idea of silence or contemplative practice is a foreign concept so I am trying to bring it in really gently. I am going to be taking it further this term. I am about to co-lead a group with a counsellor on pastoral care and we will bookend the weekly sessions with silence or some form of contemplative practice.

A COMMON CONCERN, PARTICULARLY FROM SOME IN THE EVANGELICAL CHURCH, HAS BEEN THAT CONTEMPLATIVE PRACTICE IS ROOTED IN BUDDHISM. HAVE YOU ENCOUNTERED THOSE CONCERNS, AND WHERE DO YOU SIT WITH THAT?
We need to clearly communicate that this is centred on Jesus and use it as a space to focus on Jesus. It's about sitting with God; listening and sensing God.

SOME PEOPLE FIND CONTEMPLATIVE PRACTICE TRICKY. HAVE YOU FOUND ANYTHING THAT WORKS FOR YOU?
Creating enough space, when we live stressful lives, is going to take us a while. I practise it each morning. I set a timer on my phone; it's a discipline. The longer I have done it, the more I desire it. The longer you can give it the better; it can't be rushed. The end of the day can be good too; the Examen is a good practice. There are some practices where they encourage you to take time in the morning, midday

and evening; these are good, they help you to be conscious of God all the time.

REFLECTION ON THIS CONVERSATION

I have had a few conversations with Flic during the last year about contemplative practice. We live in the same village and discovered we shared this common interest. I really value Flic's thoughts on the discipline of making time for this in our busy lives. She is a busy working mum with three young children. Finding time to put aside 10 minutes each day is not always easy, but she has found a way to incorporate those 10 minutes at the start of each day into a routine. I also love how, despite us both coming from very different parts of the church family, we have found a common thread and a shared language and understanding that we can support and encourage each other in.

CONCLUSION

By using stillness, silence and meditation in our prayer life we are re-finding the golden thread that has been handed to us through the long Christian history. I sometimes wonder if some of the fear around this practice comes out of the difficulty people have with it. In many ways this is not an easy practice; maybe it is harder for us today, at this current time, in our frenetic, 'doing' society to stop and find stillness. But as O'Rourke (2011) suggests, we need to put trust in the silence and through that trust know that God is in the silence.

SUGGESTIONS FOR FURTHER READING ON CONTEMPLATIVE PRACTICE

Adams, I. (2010) *Cave Refectory Road: Monastic Rhythms for Contemporary Living.* London: Canterbury Press.

Adams, I. (2013) *Running over Rocks: Spiritual Practices to Transform Tough Times.* London: Canterbury Press.

Laird, M. (2006) *Into the Silent Land: The Practice of Contemplation.* New York: Oxford University Press.

Laird, M. (2011) *A Sunlit Absence.* New York: Oxford University Press.

O'Rourke, B. (2011) *Finding Your Hidden Treasure: The Way of Silent Prayer.* Liguori, MI: Liguori Publications

REFERENCES

Adams, I. (2010) *Cave Refectory Road: Monastic Rhythms for Contemporary Living.* London: Canterbury Press.

Adams, I. (2013) *Running over Rocks: Spiritual Practices to Transform Tough Times.* London: Canterbury Press.

Barrington-Ward, S. (1996) *The Jesus Prayer.* Oxford: The Bible Reading Fellowship.

Jamison, C. (2006) *Finding Sanctuary: Monastic Steps for Everyday Life.* London: Weidenfeld and Nicolson.

Laird, M. (2006) *Into the Silent Land: The Practice of Contemplation.* New York: Oxford University Press.

Laird, M. (2011) *A Sunlit Absence.* New York: Oxford University Press.

Merton, T. (2005) *The Pocket Thomas Merton* (edited by Robert Inchausti). London: New Seeds Books.

O'Rourke, B. (2011) *Finding Your Hidden Treasure: The Way of Silent Prayer.* Liguori, MI: Liguori Publications

Stead, T. (2018) *See, Love, Be: Mindfulness and the Spiritual Life.* London: SPCK.

Ward, B. (2003) *The Desert Fathers: Sayings of the Early Christian Monks.* London: Penguin Books.

Section 2

Practice Ideas
and Suggestions

CHAPTER 4

USING OUTDOOR SPACES

How often do you use outdoor spaces as a place to pray or worship? Years ago I realised I feel most in touch with God when I am outside, particularly in wild places: the beach, the sea, meadows, woods, all these places help me feel connected to God. Personally, I rarely encounter God in a building. I know that many do, and that is great, but there also many like me, especially children, who feel God's presence more when they are outside. This section is not suggesting you don't spend any time inside; however, I would encourage you to try some of these ideas. The gospels are full of examples of Jesus choosing to take himself off to pray on the mountain, on the beach and so on. Being outside reminds me of the awesomeness of God's creation.

I have used outdoor spaces a lot in various worship and children's work; this chapter will offer a range of ideas that you can try. Some of these work as a short exercise to carry out with different sized groups of children. Others are examples of how you do the whole service or group outside. Please do adapt them for your group. As I mention in the introduction to this section, it is important that the adults join in and take part in all the activities you are doing;

all these ideas are to be carried out alongside children. By doing this with the children you are modelling and scaffolding their experience.

Over the years I have seen children across the ages respond very positively to outdoor spaces. Children and young people are often drawn to the awe and wonder around them; they notice, they value and they sense God's presence within creation. Too often we presume that children and young people prefer to be indoors, on technology, but often when we give them the opportunity to engage with nature they will willingly do so. In the same way we can underestimate how children and young people can feel close to God through being in nature.

LISTENING WALK (ALL AGES)

This can be done in any outdoor space. I often use this exercise with the 4-year-olds I work with in my nurture work, getting them to really listen and notice what sounds are around them. With children in a church context, you can then take this on further and talk about how this can be a prayerful walk, how it can be a way of listening to God.

This activity is a good way to help children really listen, to be aware of and engage with the wonderful creation around them. It is a good activity to help them be mindful and notice. It is a great way of introducing a contemplative practice and can help to calm an anxious or overactive child.

Find a space to walk; this may be around a garden, in some woods, on a beach, in a park or along a road.

Tell the child/group that you are all going to be listening very carefully, listening to all the different sounds. Tell them that for this walk to work, they will all need to be very quiet.

Explain this can be a prayerful walk: as they walk and listen, their attention may be taken by something they want to pray for or give thanks for.

At the end of the walk ask them what sounds they heard. You could ask them what the sounds helped them think of or how the sounds made them feel. You could ask, 'What has God said to you today through the sounds you heard?'

PLANTING AND PRAYING (AGE 4 AND OVER)

This is a prayerful exercise that I have used many times with children across the age range. It is a practical way to use help children use contemplative practice and thoughts about new beginnings.

You will need:

- plant pots or a flowerbed
- bag of compost
- seeds or bulbs
- watering can.

For this exercise you may want to find some Bible verses that are relevant to what you are doing. Another way to use this is as a prayer exercise, for instance at the beginning of a new school year.

Ask your group to think in silence about the new term, new school year or new experiences ahead of them. Get them to think about their hopes and worries for the time ahead.

Invite them to plant a seed or a bulb to represent themselves at the start of this new term/year and then add water to this.

As you draw this to an end the leader can pray over the seeds: for God to help these bulbs and seeds to grow over the coming year, and for each member of the group to grow.

You can either send the pots home with the children and encourage them to water them, or, if they are planted in the church garden or a flowerbed, make sure they get watered over the year.

NATURE CARDS (ALL AGES)

Ian Adams in *Running over Rocks* (2013) has an exercise which I love called Terra Divina; his exercise works really well with older children and teenagers. If you are not familiar with this, I would urge you read the book and try the exercise. The Terra Divina exercise is about being outside, walking and noticing, seeing what captures your attention, seeing this as a gift and how God is speaking to you through this gift. I have adapted Ian's Terra Divina to work across the age range. This prayerful, contemplative walk is an exercise we have used at different times to the year in our Forest Church, capturing the different colours throughout the year.

It is an accessible way to help children begin using Terra Divina, which later links to Lectio Divina. This is a mindful and contemplative exercise which can help to calm anxious or agitated children. It can also help to engage children with the creation around them.

You will need:

- small pieces of card, postcard size works well
- double-sided sticky tape covering the card in strips
- a space or area to walk and explore – a park, a garden, woods, beach, for example.

We used this activity in Sanctuary during a prayer walk around the streets and canal that the church was situated in. If you are in an enclosed, safe space then allow children to wander and do this by themselves, but also make sure you and the other adults do it as well. You will find children are often naturally silent as they are in the moment and enjoyment of this exercise.

Make sure everyone has their own card.

At the start of this activity encourage everyone to walk and really notice what is around them, notice what God has designed and created.

Encourage the children to touch and smell as well as look, really engaging all their senses. Explain that you are going to be taking a prayer nature walk. Ask the children to find objects which remind them of God and stick these on their card. This might be a feather, leaf, flower petal or shell for instance. They can pick as many things as they want or they may choose to put just one thing on; this is open ended.

At the end it is great to have a look at everyone's pictures; they will all be totally different. You could invite the group to talk about how they saw God today, what reminded them of God, what most excited them and how this made them feel.

PRAYER WALK (ALL AGES)

Every October in Sanctuary we would take a prayer walk for our service. This involved walking around the neighbourhood and praying for the area. We did this exercise with all ages. Tony Cook (who was interviewed in Chapter 1) has done this exercise with his youth group, walking around the city where their church is located.

This is a good exercise for helping children to pray for their surroundings and what is happening in their community.

You will need:

- an agreed walking route.

Gather together in an agreed area. Explain to the group that you are going to be walking and praying for the area.

Ask the children/young people to be aware of the buildings and what is on the streets as they walk; ask them to think about whether there is one thing that took their attention. Ideally, this exercise works well in silence, with everyone silently praying for the area, but it can also be done while having conversations. Just remind people to notice if one thing stands out to them.

When you have ended the walk, gather back together and talk about what they noticed, what came to their attention. Ask how did God speak to them? Was there anything that moved them? Is there any way they or the group can respond to some of the things they saw?

This works across the ages and much younger children could also do the nature card idea. What I love about this exercise is the way children really notice things that as adults we may overlook. The one thing they may notice and want to pray about may be an animal or some broken toys or the amount of dog poo or broken glass. Then when you discuss about how you can respond, they often have some excellent and practical ideas.

This exercise can be useful to do for a church to help them think about the needs of their community. On the back of this exercise you may discover things you didn't know and notice needs that you may be able to support as a church. This exercise could feed into parish/church plans for the area; it is a very practical and positive way to involve children and young people in this and to listen to their ideas.

QUIET GARDENS (ALL AGES)

There is a growing interest in quiet gardens; these are garden spaces which have been set up for prayer, reflection and rest. A number of schools, churches, hospitals and retreat centres have these and some are in private gardens. A growing number of schools are setting up quiet gardens, recognising how they can help children to find some stillness and calm amidst the busyness of a school day. Some of the quiet gardens run quiet days and retreat days. There is a Quiet Garden Movement website[1] dedicated to this practice where you find out about the quiet gardens near to you and events in these gardens. You may want to consider having a quiet garden in your church or school.

FORAGING (ALL AGES)

Over the years I have become a big fan of foraging: finding free food and making things from this. This started for me from a trip to a kindergarten in Denmark situated on the edge of woodland. While there I observed how the children knew what it was okay to pick and eat and what they couldn't. The children, aged 2 to 6 years, were really connected with the creation around them. This experience helped me to reflect on how disconnected from nature so many children are today. Foraging as part of your worship time and then cooking and sharing the food can be an excellent practice. In Sanctuary, around autumn, we often foraged for blackberries and then made a pie or crumble to share. At other times we made bread together in the service, putting into it herbs we had grown in

---

[1]   https://quietgarden.org

the garden. In Forest Church we often forage; we are not often able to cook the food, although it is possible to do some basic cooking on a fire. Most months we bring food and drink to share as part of the service that we have previously foraged and then made. This month I brought blackberry muffins and warm elderberry and blackberry cordial, which was perfect for that service as the day we met it was pouring with rain. The act of sharing and tasting the food of the woodlands was a wonderful way to connect us to the God who created them. The act of foraging is very contemplative and mindful, as you are carefully thinking about what you are doing: looking, smelling and carefully picking. Below are a few ideas of how you could use foraging. This, of course, comes with a warning to make sure you know what you are foraging. You must explain to the children that they are only to do this activity with an adult. Personally I would never forage for fungi as I am not knowledgeable about these, and there are risks to health if you get it wrong.

This is good exercise to help children begin on the mindful, contemplative journey. It gives them something very clear to focus on and the process of foraging gets us to engage with the wonderful creation around us.

WILD GARLIC (EARLY SPRING TIME)
For this activity you need to be in a space where wild garlic is growing; where I live it grows abundantly in the lanes and woods.

Show the children what wild garlic looks like. Have a piece to show them; get them to smell and taste it.

Get the children to find wild garlic leaves to pick, reminding them not to pull out the bulbs and not to pick all the leaves in one area.

Remind the children to notice what they are doing; notice what is around the garlic; notice the smell and feel of the leaves.

You could talk about which animals might eat this food and how the bulbs split and extend to grow more plants over the years.

Encourage the children to think about how diverse the food is that we can eat.

When you go back to your building you could make:

- Wild garlic soda bread: I like Jack Munro's soda bread recipe on her cooking blog Cooking on boot strap.[2] Just add the chopped wild garlic into the dough mix.

- Wild garlic soup: I really like the wild garlic and nettle soup recipe from BBC Good Food website.[3] For the nettle leaves, always pick young leaves and wear gardening gloves!

- Wild garlic pesto: the recipe I use for this is from Woodland Trust website.[4] They also have tips on this page about how to forage for wild garlic.

---

[2] https://cookingonabootstrap.com/2018/10/02/soda-bread-recipe-2/

[3] www.bbcgoodfood.com/recipes/wild-garlic-nettle-soup

[4] www.woodlandtrust.org.uk/blog/2017/02/how-to-forage-wild-garlic-and-make-wild-garlic-pesto

The act of making food together and then eating together is a wonderful communal activity. As you are making food together, encourage the children to think about where the food came from, how it grew, the smells, the tastes. You could link this to the creation story.

You could also encourage the children to think about the type of food that would have been around in biblical times – where they would have found the food; how they gathered the food.

Making food and then eating together can be a very mindful, contemplative process. As you share it, remember to give thanks for the food you have found and cooked with. You could get the children to write a prayer or some liturgy around this theme.

ELDERFLOWER (MAY)
You can make elderflower cordial; there is a recipe on BBC Good Food.[5]

MUSSELS ON THE BEACH
You forage these in months with an 'r' in them. Steam them or boil them – you could eat them on the beach. Only eat mussels where the shells have opened in the water as you cooked them.

---

[5]   www.bbcgoodfood.com/recipes/531660/homemade-elderflower-cordial

USING OUTDOOR SPACES

ELDERBERRIES AND BLACKBERRIES (END OF SUMMER/AUTUMN)

You can make pies and crumbles and cordials with these. An elderberry cordial recipe I use is from a website called 'eat weeds'[6] and I sometimes add blackberries to this.

REFERENCE

Adams, I. (2013) *Running over Rocks: Spiritual Practices to Transform Tough Times.* London: Canterbury Press.

---

[6] www.eatweeds.co.uk/elderberry-cordial-syrup

CHAPTER 5

USING MEDITATIONS

Using meditations with children can be a really useful tool to help them experience some stillness. The Mindfulness in Schools Project[1] and the Meditation with Children Project in Ireland[2] use meditations. These are often with children in upper primary and secondary schools, but there are also secular resources for younger children using meditation practices. Relax Kids[3] is a very good one, using stories as the basis of the meditation. To start with meditations are often spoken – guided meditation – with, some words to listen to but lots of space around the words. This helps children and adults to get used to sitting in stillness, and the words can help them to focus on something. As you develop using meditations, you may end up using fewer words and then eventually you may just sit in silence and meditate on a word or a picture. However, it's okay to come back to using some words when you are finding the complete silence too hard. In my experience there will be times when you need to go back to the guided meditations, and that is fine.

---

[1]   https://mindfulnessinschools.org

[2]   http://christianmeditation.ie/?q=meditationwithchildren

[3]   www.relaxkids.com/Default.aspx

The general advice on using meditations with children is that you use a practice with one minute per age, so a 5-year-old would be able to do a 5-minute practice. In my experience, if you have been practising this for a while a lot of children can manage longer. Noel Keating (2017) believes that meditation is a very ordinary practice to children. He suggests that once they are used to the practice they often enjoy its simplicity and happily use it regularly, but to start with keep it short. In the meditations he uses with children, he guides them to use a prayer word or mantra (as was mentioned by Father Christopher in the interview in Chapter 3). The word he often uses with children is 'Maranatha'.

Below are some different ways to use meditation practice. I would suggest that before you use any of these practices with children you become familiar with them yourself. Also, when you using these exercises with children make sure you do them alongside them.

MEDITATION WITH VISUALS (AGE 3 AND OVER)

This is a method I have used in a lot of different situations over the years, with groups of children and as part of an all-age service.

This exercise is a simple early introduction to using meditations; it enables you to start using silent, meditative practice in a carefully curated way.

You will need:

- bean bags/cushions/blankets on the floor
- visuals on a screen.

Explain to the group that you are going to be listening to some words. Encourage the group to sit or lie on the floor.

Explain that there are also some pictures to look at as well as listening to the words and that they may prefer to lie with their eyes closed, or they may like to sit up and look at the pictures as well as listen to the words.

Slowly read the words of your meditation and have an appropriate visual on the screen; for example, if I was using a meditation about creation, I would ensure that my images were of creation.

HOW TO WRITE GUIDED MEDITATIONS

There are meditations available in books or online but it is great if you can write your own, or encourage the children to be involved in writing them. You could use a poem, a prayer or some words from the Bible as the basis of your meditation. My tips for writing a meditation for children are as follows:

- Keep it short.

- Use words they will understand.

- Use words that help create an image; for example, walking along a beach and how the sand feels under their feet or picking a flower and thinking about the colour and the smell.

- Talk them through what you want them to do; for example, 'lie on your back, put your hand on your belly, notice your breathing'. This puts them in a good place to start a meditation.

MEDITATION IN SILENCE (AGE 4 AND OVER)

At first, meditating in silence can feel odd and we can often be worried that children will not want to engage in this, but I have found that a lot of children are open to trying it out for short periods of time. This exercise is a very simple introduction to starting contemplative practice and experiencing times of silent prayer.

You will need:

- a timer to start and end the meditation: you can use an app on your phone or iPad for this; it saves you watching the clock.

Explain that we are going to sit and be with God for a few minutes, in silence. Remind the children that God is there with them in the silence.

First, talk about how often when we sit in silence our minds can be full of lots of thoughts and ideas and that is okay, God doesn't mind. You could use a 'calming bottle' as an example of how our minds can be (see the recipe below).

Encourage the children to close their eyes, put their hands on their bellies and notice their breath moving in and out.

Encourage them to notice what they can hear around them.

Remind them that if thoughts come into their head that is fine, just notice the breathing.

At first keep this to around 3 minutes; as you do the exercise more, you can slowly increase the duration. You can remind children that they can use this at any time in the day. Remind them that if there are times in the day when they are feeling cross, upset or are finding things hard, they can close their eyes and do a short meditation to help them feel calmer and more peaceful.

Calming bottle

This is similar to a snow globe. If possible make this with the child.

Pour some glitter into the bottom of an empty plastic bottle. Fill the bottle with water and add one teaspoon of glycerine.

Attach the lid and securely tighten (glue on if possible).

Shake the bottle and all the glitter will fizz around. Explain that sometimes this is how our minds and our tummies can feel. Watch as the glitter slowly calms. Get the child to put one hand on their tummy and one on their heart. Ask them to breathe slowly as they are watching the glitter settle. Explain that our minds and tummies can be like the glitter, with lots of thoughts and feelings going fast. As we meditate and breathe slowly, our mind and tummy can begin to calm and we can begin to feel calmer.

MEDITATION USING A PRAYER WORD (AGE 5 AND OVER)

In Chapter 3, Father Christopher from Downside talks about using a word mantra as a meditation. This is also the main type of meditation that is used by Noel Keating (2017) in the Meditation with Children Project. Father Christopher talks about using the word 'Maranatha', which means 'Come Lord Jesus.' The other type of prayer word or phrase often used is the Jesus Prayer; Mother Sarah refers to this in Chapter 3 as the main prayer in the Orthodox tradition. The words for this are: 'Lord Jesus Christ Son of God have mercy on...' This is a good exercise for children who find sitting in silence tricky. For this exercise you are still in engaging in a stillness practice, but you have words, in your mind, to focus on. This method can also help to bring calmness to the child. You could use this exercise at the end of the day, before bed; it would be a calming, contemplative way to end the day. I know some families who use this together as part of their bedtime routine.

You will need:

- a timer to start and end the meditation.

Encourage the group/child to sit in a comfortable position, usually with their back straight and feet on the ground.

Ask them to close their eyes.

Suggest to them that they slowly repeat the word in their heads – 'Ma-ra-na-tha' – saying each part on separate breaths; for example:

Ma – inhalation
Ra – exhalation
Na – inhalation.
Tha – exhalation.

For the first few times of using the meditation, set a timer for between 3 and 5 minutes.

MEDITATION TOOLS

There is a Christian app with guided meditations called 'Meaningful'[4], written by a Christian woman called Olivia. You could use these with older children (age 7 and over) in a group, individually or as a family. These are lovely to use.

Mark Yaconelli (2010) has written an excellent book called *Wonder, Fear and Longing*; this is a book of prayers with meditations and contemplative practices to use. I really like this book; I think the prayers and practices in it will work across a wide age range. You may need to adapt some for the age of your group, but I believe most people will find something they can use to support them and their group. Mark is writing it from a place of encouragement to find stillness and silence in your prayer practice.

REFERENCES

Keating, N. (2017) *Meditation with Children: A Resource for Teachers and Parents*. Dublin: Veritas.

Yaconelli, M. (2010) *Wonder, Fear and Longing: A Book of Prayers*. London: SPCK.

---

4   www.meaningfulapp.com

CHAPTER 6

USING MOVEMENT

I mentioned in an earlier chapter that some adults and children find that sitting still can be very difficult. My youngest daughter has dyspraxia and sensory processing difficulties, and she can find a sitting meditation incredibly challenging and frustrating. I firmly believe that we can pray through movement and moving prayer can help you come to a place of stillness within you. My friend Ian Adams runs daily and describes his running as a body prayer. As I mentioned in an earlier chapter, I swim daily and my swimming is a prayerful exercise for me; within the movement I am able to find some inner stillness and silence. Below are some examples of how you can use movement and prayer to find stillness.

LABYRINTH (ALL AGES)

Labyrinths are circular walking pathways; they have been used as an ancient practice of circling to the centre and praying, with links that back 4000 years. Labyrinths are a one-path design in a circle shape, with one entrance and exit. They are often used as a meditation tool or a prayer tool; they are sometimes described as a walking prayer or a walking meditation.[1] You can find labyrinths in churches, cathedrals, retreat centres, schools and universities, and some public spaces. A list of some of the labyrinths in the UK can be found on the 'Pilgrims Paths' website.[2] You can make your own labyrinth. Some people mow a temporary one on grass, others use rope or pebbles and I have seen some on beaches. You can also make a more permanent structure with stones, gravel or willow. Labyrinths work well across the ages.

This exercise is a lovely way to intentionally use walking and prayer together. If you are new to contemplative practices, this can be a good place to start. Having a path to follow gives you a structure, children often enjoy the act of following a pathway, and they often understand and appreciate the act of doing this work slowly, mindfully and prayerfully.

You will need:

- a labyrinth – one created already or your own made from rope, pebbles or sand.

Explain to the children that you are using the labyrinth as a prayer walk.

Invite them to walk around the path.

Explain that they may want to start the walk by thinking about how this is a chance to walk with God.

---

[1]   https://sacredwalk.com/guidelines
[2]   www.pilgrimpaths.co.uk/page21.html

The walk to the centre can be a time of letting go of their worries, thoughts and fears.

When they are at the centre, they can lift these to God and let in God's love.

As they walk back, they know that God has heard them and is with them.

Or:

Encourage them to walk the path slowly as a prayer; by walking they are praying and don't need any words or thoughts. The act of walking in this space is a prayer.

Some people also use finger labyrinths as a meditation/movement tool at home; again these are described on the Pilgrim Paths website. A photo of one my husband[3] carved is below.

---

[3]   http://iaincotton.co.uk

BODY PRAYER (ALL AGES)

I have used body prayer in different situations, as part of an all-age service, with small groups of children and on my own. Each time I use this, I play a piece of ambient music without words, and I use three simple words and signs. The aim of this prayer is to repeat the prayer without voicing the words, instead signing the prayer.

The words and their signs are as follows:

Come

Lord

Jesus

This is a good exercise to use when people find the act of sitting too difficult.

You will need:

- ambient music without words.

Introduce the words and signs you are using.

Invite the children to copy your actions, with the ambient music in the background (or you could do this is silence).

Repeat the words/signs slowly and rhythmically for a few minutes. By repeating this, you enter into the prayer.

You can make up your own words and signs, or use signs that are specific to British Sign Language or Makaton. A lovely activity is to create this with the children, with them choosing the words and signs to use.

Ian and Gail Adams have created a body prayer to the Beatitudes which can be found on their 'beloved life' website.[4] Their prayer would work well across all ages.

BUBBLE PRAYERS (ALL AGES)

These have become a firm favourite of mine. In Sanctuary they became such an integral part of our worship that my children were very confused if they were in a mainstream church service and bubbles were not being used! We used bubble prayers for intercessions, at weddings, funerals, christenings or any celebration. Bubble prayers are very visual representations of our prayers.

You will need:

- pots of bubbles – small pots for party bags are excellent and cheap to buy.

If possible, hand out a pot of bubbles to every person in the group; if you don't have enough then encourage them to share.

Explain that in the Orthodox Church, they use incense to take their prayers to God and that we are using bubbles to take the prayers to God.

Encourage everyone to pray silently and then blow their prayers to God.

There is something very beautiful in seeing bubbles floating in the sky, knowing these symbolise many prayers. We now use bubble prayers each time we meet

---

[4]   www.belovedlife.org/beloved-life-body-prayer-the-beatitudes

in Forest Church, I have recently started using giant bubbles as part of this. We all have a small pot first and then I explain that we have some giant bubble mix for the really big prayers we have, and people come up one at a time to make the giant prayer bubble. Your can buy a giant bubble wand cheaply or make your own; look on Pinterest[5] for instructions. This is the recipe I use for making my own giant bubble mixture (this can also be used as a refill in your bubble pots):

- six cups of water
- one cup of strong washing up liquid (not an eco one, as they don't work so well)
- one tablespoon of liquid glycerin (you can buy from the baking aisle of a supermarket).

Gently mix together, trying not to make bubbles. Dip your giant bubble wand in the mixture and gently move your hands apart, and move slowly to make the bubble (this may take some practice).

BAREFOOT WALKING (ALL AGES)

Before you do this, you will need to risk assess the outdoor space you are going to use, making sure there is no broken glass for instance. You could do this exercise on a patch of grass, a beach, a wooded area, a muddy area or even a car park. Each space will have its own feel and textures. You may want bowls of water and towels at the end if people need them to clean up.

---

[5]   www.pinterest.co.uk

The act of barefoot walking slows you down; it almost forces you to become very present and mindful. Barefoot walking also really connects you to the ground and the earth and, in turn, to God, who created it. I find barefoot walking is a lovely connecting and contemplative exercise. It works particularly well when children are agitated or stressed. There is something about feeling the grass or sand under their feet that often calms children, and it can be a good way to introduce contemplative practice to children. Having said that, some children may have sensory processing issues and find this a distressing idea; if this is the case, suggest they walk but with their socks on.

You will need:

- an outside space – for example grass, beach or woodland
- bowls of water and towels if appropriate.

Bring everyone outside.

Explain that you are going to do some barefoot walking. Encourage everyone to take off their shoes and socks. Tell everyone how long you are doing this for. If this is the first time, keep it to 5 minutes. Explain that this is a time to walk slowly and that they will be using this as a prayer.

Explain that this is a time where they are invited to walk and notice and pray, if possible praying without words. Tell the children that their walk will be their prayer. You can suggest that they start by saying in their head 'Lord hear my prayer.'

Say something along the lines of, 'As you walk notice how it feels, notice what you see and smell and hear, notice how this makes you feel.'

After 5 minutes, bring the activity to an end and discuss how the children found this.

This exercise works with children on a one-to-one basis, as a family, with a small group or a bigger group. I regularly come back to the exercise myself, particularly when I am feeling overwhelmed. This morning, writing this section, I have been feeling particularly anxious and full of self-doubt. I write from a small office/shed at the bottom of my garden. Before I started writing today, I knew I needed to barefoot walk around our community meadow, which is at the back of my office. I knew I would find this exercise calming and grounding and it enabled to me to feel held by God. Barefoot walking forces you to slow down, notice, be aware, be mindful. Give it a go.

CHAPTER 7

USING ART
AND CREATIVITY

I think church groups have lost the way they engage with the arts and creativity. As I mentioned in an earlier chapter, quite a lot of churches often use ready-made template craft activities with children, but rarely engage in other forms of creativity. In Sanctuary, many in the community were artists, including my husband. Exploring how we integrated the arts and creativity into our worship was a key element in what we did and intentionally considering how this worked with children was an important element in our thinking. For much of the church's history, people were illiterate and visual images were a really important way to bring the Bible to life for them: churches were filled with stained glass, wall paintings and carvings. Churches were also patrons of artists. In some churches images are still a vital part of the service; this is particularly seen in the Orthodox Church, with its beautiful Icons. I believe we need to re-engage with the arts in our worship. Thinking about how they were used to open up the Bible and the stories to people who couldn't read is a good way for us to see how we can use art with children today. Below are some ideas to try.

PRAYER AND FELTING (AGE 3 AND OVER)

This is an activity one of our group members called Gwyneth Evans set up as part of one of the Examen questions, but we also used it in other services. The act of felting is a very calming, contemplative one. This activity is based around felting a pebble, enabling a conversation with God beyond words. It elicits the questions: 'What reached me today?' and 'How deep did it imprint?'

I have used it with children of different ages. They often love the way the wool fibres change from loose fibres to being felted together. In this activity you are moving the pebble over and over in your hand, which is rhythmic and soothing. It also works really well as a prayerful activity, allowing your actions to become a prayerful act. This is an activity that works well for children who find sitting still hard and it also works well as an introduction to a contemplative, prayerful act.

You will need:

- pebbles
- two colours of felting wool (you can buy this online)
- a squirt of washing up liquid or soap
- warm water.

Ask the children to find a pebble and two colours of wool, choosing one colour to represent God for them today and another for themselves.

They should fan out the fibres lengthways, blending the two colours and making a band of fibres roughly the width of the stone and eight times its length.

Then they need to cocoon the pebble with the band of fibres, wrapping it lengthwise and widthwise in many directions, making sure the whole pebble is covered.

Ask them to cradle the pebble in the palm of one hand, thoroughly wetting it in the soapy water, then squeeze out the excess. They should then gently massage it in a circular motion with the fingertips of the other hand for 10 minutes or so.

Whilst felting the pebble, ask the children to pay attention to all of the stone, remembering that God loves all aspects of us and our conversation with him will encompass our whole lives. The children should notice, too, the felt shrinking to the contours of the pebble as the fibres meld together. Ask them to reflect on how God's gracious love covers us and uses our imperfections to make something beautiful.

Ask the children, when they feel the felting process has begun, to look at the colours to see how they have blended together to make a material – to note how their colour enhances the colour of God and the colour of God brings out the beauty of their colour. The children should continue to roll the pebble between their palms, making the felt, and see what God says to them.

They can then rinse off the soapy solution in hot water, which helps the felting process further, and allow it to dry.

The children can use the felted stone as a prayer aid and take it home as a reminder of conversations with God beyond words.

PRAYER BEADS (ALL AGES)

I have made prayer beads with several different groups of children of all ages. This prayer beads exercise is influenced by the Rosary, which is often used in the Catholic tradition. Children love making these; the exercise allows them space to be creative, to make something that represents things that are important to them. The beads are made from Fimo®. It works well for this as you can easily mould it, mix colours and, once baked in the oven, it lasts. Once you have made the prayer beads everyone can take them home and use them in their contemplative prayer time. This is a lovely activity to do as a group and can work well in an all-age service. There is something beautiful about sitting around a large table together creating these beads, the adults and children supporting one another. If you have younger children in the group, they may need some support in making the beads, but make sure you find out from the children what their ideas are and how they would like support, rather than doing it for them.

This exercise encourages the children to think about what is in their life that they are thankful for. There is no right or wrong way to make a bead; you can make it look like something, or it can be a colour to represent something; it can be any shape or size. The act of making the beads can be contemplative and reflective. Once you have made the beads you can use them as a prayer aid, moving your hands over each individual bead and giving thanks for what the bead represents.

You will need:

- Fimo® of different colours (you can buy this from craft shops or online)
- cutters and blunt knives
- a needle to make a hole in the beads
- thread for the beads.

Tell the children they are going to use the Fimo® to make some prayer beads which represent different areas of their lives that they want to give thanks for; this might be school, home, toys, outdoor spaces, family, friends, play or anything else.

When they have finished the beads, they need to make a hole in them and thread them onto the string.

They will need to cook these when they get home at 110°C or 230°F for 30 minutes.

Ask the children to give thanks to God for the things in their life that these beads represent.

STATIONS OF THE CROSS (AGE 4 AND OVER)

Stations of the Cross are a common tool used by Catholics. I am currently working in a Catholic primary school and they have beautiful small bronze relief sculptures of the stations along the corridors. The Stations of the Cross are a fantastic way to help children visualise and think about the Easter story. Over a few years in Sanctuary we explored the Stations of the Cross at Easter. Some years we each made a station to explore as a group; other years we put on exhibitions. One year we created an exhibition called 'Passion Postcards'; we used large banners made from polystyrene, each one representing one of the Stations of the Cross; for example, Jesus meets his mother. We invited people of all ages – artists and non-artists – to create a postcard-sized piece of art to go on one of the stations so each hanging block had different images to represent that Station of the Cross: see the photograph below.

Later that year we took this idea to Greenbelt Christian Arts festival, and set it up as an installation for people to add to over the weekend. We took thousands of postcards for people of all ages to design their passion postcards along with chalks, pens, pencils, charcoal and pastels. Festival goers were invited to look at the exhibition and then make their own pieces of artwork to go alongside the exhibition.

The beauty of this exhibition was that it involved everyone of all ages in our community and it also involved people from outside of our community, both those of faith and those with no faith. The work was carefully curated to look beautiful; this was a show with both professional artists' work alongside that of non-artists and children. There was a beauty and simplicity in this idea. Over the weekend at Greenbelt, thousands of people came to see the exhibition and to add their piece of artwork.

What I loved about this exhibition was the way children of all ages were able to participate in it and understand it. Each station clearly explained what it was and the children were able to respond in whatever they wanted. I observed that children found the visual narrative of the stations a helpful way to engage and partake. This activity was not just about artists making artwork: it was an encouragement to us all to respond in a creative way, recognising we all have creative gifts.

Have a list of the stations you want to use, you can find lists with an online search (there are 14, you may choose to use fewer).

You will need:

- a rich mix of art materials, for example, chalks, pastels, charcoal, pens, pencils, glue, loose parts.

Invite everyone to create something for one of the stations.

Give time and space for everyone to create something then place each item within the station it is linked to.

Spend time exploring and praying at each station.

You could leave this up over the Easter weekend.

CITY OF PEACE (ALL AGES)

One year at Greenbelt we created an installation called 'Building the City of Peace'. This was an invitation to festival goers to think about what should be in a city of peace. We had banners introducing the idea and welcoming people, including verses from Revelation 21 about the New Jerusalem.

We had a huge open indoor space in which we put van loads of scrap material, which we bought from our local scrap store (look online to see if you have one near you, they are a fantastic source of recycled materials). In the middle of the space we put a long blue sheet to represent water. We then placed the scrap materials around the room, along with pens, glue, tape and so on. We had banners with simple instructions and the invitation to create.

This was a very open-ended, no-template model. The aim of this installation was to help people of all ages to think about what they would want in a city of peace and to create that. Over the weekend thousands of people participated: grandparents, toddlers, teenagers and parents all created alongside one another. Once they had created their item, they then chose where to put it within the city. The city grew over the weekend, with many people coming back to add to it or see how it had developed. There was such a rich mix of ideas within the city, from surfers, poetry boxes, a catwalk, a football stadium and a large angel to playgrounds, schools, houses, swimming pools and animals. The very act of creating was reflective, playful and prayerful.

The aim of this activity is to engage in a creative, playful act but also to encourage a prayerful engagement, recognising that while you are making and creating you can be doing this prayerfully.

You will need:

- a wide variety of scrap materials
- a range of art materials: glue, tape, masking tape, string, paint, pens, pencils and so on.

Give clear, simple instructions of what the theme is – keep it broad. Invite people to create what they think needs to go in the installation. Give the group time to sit with, be with and explore the finished creation. Enjoy and give thanks for the many interesting and diverse things that have been created.

SITTING WITH PIECES OF ART: ARTE DIVINA (AGE 3 AND OVER)

In Chapter 3 on using the outdoors and Chapter 8 on using words, I talk about using Lectio Divina and Terra Divina practice. These are both about reading a passage or reading the landscape and seeing how God is speaking to you through this. Ian Adams (2010 and 2013) explores these in his books. This idea is a similar one, but based on sitting with a piece of art. You could call this Arte Divina to give it a Latin name.

Over the years I have often used pieces of art with children, encouraging them to sit with, look at and contemplate the art. I encourage them to think about what might be happening in the art, what the artist might have wanted us to think or feel. Within a prayerful context, I enjoy using art with children and encouraging them to see how God might be speaking to them through the art. As Sanctuary had many artists in its community, we often used their artwork. We can be afraid to use art both as adults and with children; however, my experience is that children respond really well to seeing art. My own children grew up visiting many galleries. Below are ways you use the Arte Divina idea with children.

You will need:

- some paintings or sculptures or a mix of both (you can use pictures you have downloaded from the Internet or you could do this activity in a gallery)

- cushions or beanbags.

Choose paintings or sculptures or a mix of both; if you have more than one, place them around the room. Explain what you are doing and how it works. Put cushions or beanbags in front of the artwork, so the group can spend time sitting and looking. Encourage the group to sit and look: really look and notice.

Ask, 'What can you see that catches your attention?' 'Sit and think about this; I wonder why it catches your attention?' 'Is God talking to you in some way through this artwork? Be curious. Does it make you think or feel in a certain way?'

Encourage the children to spend some time sitting, being with God in front of this art, in quiet and stillness.

You could also have art materials available and invite the children to respond to the artwork. This is not about making something the same, but thinking of their own ideas, inspired by what they have seen.

USING PHOTOS (AGE 3 AND OVER)

Most of our phones and tablets now have cameras on them; in this digital age we are used to taking photos all the time. We can use this idea as a worship activity. This is something we often do in Forest Church, and the older children with phones often take part in this. This works in a similar way to the nature cards in Chapter 4 on using the outdoors, thinking about what captures your attention.

You will need:

- a space to walk and explore – a park, a garden, woods, beach, building or street, for example
- cameras/phones with cameras or similar (one for each child).

Take a walk with the children. Ask the children to really look and notice – ask, 'What captures your attention?' Tell the children to take a photo of this. They may want to take a few photos, but encourage them to take no more than five.

When you have finished the walk, ask the children to take a look at the photos. Ask, 'What was it that captured your attention?' Encourage them to think about how God was present in that moment.

REFERENCES

Adams, I. (2010) *Cave Refectory Road: Monastic Rhythms for Contemporary Living.* London: Canterbury Press.
Adams, I. (2013) *Running over Rocks: Spiritual Practices to Transform Tough Times.* London: Canterbury Press.

CHAPTER 8

USING WORDS

The focus of this book has been on how we can help children and young people to find stillness and contemplative practice. A lot of practices I have given are examples of ways to use fewer words or no words at all. This chapter is examples of how we can use words, but in a more spacious and contemplative way. The ideas in this chapter are aimed at children aged 7 and over, although with support younger children can access them too. The activities here are particularly useful for children who are carrying big feelings. In the first section of the book I talk about how important it is for us to support children's wellbeing; I think these activities are especially good for supporting children who are feeling angry, anxious, depressed or worried.

WRITING IN THE SAND (AGE 7 AND OVER, OR YOUNGER IF AN ADULT SUPPORTS)

I have used this activity with children of all ages, sometimes setting it up as one of a few stations for them to engage in or sometimes as a standalone activity. This activity is sensory and calming and encourages contemplative, prayerful practice.

You will need:

- a tray of sand

- pebbles or shells

- a written copy of Psalm 139 next to the tray of sand.

Have the instructions below written next to the tray:

- Read the Psalm and spend some time thinking about what God is saying to you.

- Write a prayer in the sand. When you have finished you can smooth it over if you want. Others don't need to see it.

- Take away a pebble or shell with you to remind you of this moment and your prayer.

WRITING YOUR OWN PSALMS (AGE 7 AND OVER, OR YOUNGER IF AN ADULT SUPPORTS)

I have used this as an activity on its own or as above as part of a selection of stations. It encourages creativity and reflective and contemplative practice.

You will need:

- Bibles

- pens

- paper

- cushions to sit on.

Explain to the children that the Psalms are full of ways people cried out to God and told him how they were feeling. Say something along the lines of: 'Sometimes it can be hard to express how we really feel. The Psalms show us it is okay to tell God how we are feeling –whether it is anger, frustration, sadness, depression or happiness, these feelings are all okay.'

Ask the children to take some time to look at some of the Psalms. Ask, 'Are there ones that relate to how you feel right now?'

Encourage the children to spend some time writing their own Psalm. Stress that it doesn't have to be a perfect piece of writing, but it is an opportunity for them to sit, in silence, being honest about how they feel.

The children can take this away with them at the end.

WRITING/DRAWING IN THE MUD (ALL AGES)

This is an outside activity; it is suited to the beach as well as on a patch of earth. It is a very sensory activity and works particularly well if children are carrying big feelings. It encourages the child to be able to express those big feelings and know it is okay to feel them and give these to God.

You will need:

- a large patch of soil or space on a beach

- sticks.

Say something along the lines of the following:

Sometimes life can feel hard and difficult and our feelings can be big; maybe you feel angry, or mad, or really sad. These feelings are okay. When we feel like this it is good to express these feelings, but in a way which won't hurt anyone. God wants to hear these big feelings. Take a stick and draw or write your feelings. You may want to write words and you may want to draw a picture, or you may just want to scribble away in the mud or sand. This is your chance to express exactly how you feel. When you have finished, know that God has seen and heard your thoughts.

WRITING AND BURNING YOUR THOUGHTS/ FEARS (AGE 4 AND OVER; ADULT SUPPORT IS ESSENTIAL IN THIS)

You will need:

- paper
- pens
- vessel to safely burn paper in – fire pits are excellent.

Ask the children to take some time thinking about the things that are on their minds right now. These may be things that scare them, worry them or make them anxious.

Ask them to write or draw these thoughts, then fold the paper over so no one else can see what they have written.

Say something along the lines of: 'We are now going to burn these papers. By burning them we are offering to God, knowing that he will hold these for us.'

LECTIO DIVINA (AGE 7 AND OVER)

This is an ancient way of engaging with the Bible. It is a process of reading and engaging with the text. Ian Adams (2010) describes this process and offers it as a spiritual practice in his book *Cave Refectory Road*. This is mainly a practice you would use with slightly older children.

You will need:

• a passage from the Bible, written out for all to see (for children keep this passage fairly short, maybe five or seven lines).

Read out the passage, if possible using two different voices.

Ask the group to read and listen to the passage. Ask: 'Is there a word or a phrase that you really notice?' Sit and think about this word or phrase, allowing the word or phrase to become a prayer for you.

Sit in silence in God's presence for a few moments.

At the end you could ask the group what word stood out for them and if they know why this might be important for them.

In many ways this exercise is quite an intellectual exercise, and I would recommend that when doing this with children, you keep it to around 3 to 5 minutes. However, there is no reason why children cannot engage with this. Children are curious and imaginative and in many ways they can find the process of engaging with a text like this easier than adults.

LOVING KINDNESS (ALL AGES)

An exercise that is often used in mindfulness is called loving kindness. This is about being kind to yourself and saying kind words to yourself. This comes out of a practice of self-compassion. For adults, there are two excellent writers on self-compassion: Brené Brown (2015) and Kristin Neff (2011). I believe that self-compassion is something God wants for all of us. We know that we are loved by God, but we are not always loved by ourselves. Teaching children the skills of self-compassion and self-love is crucial to their wellbeing and mental health. The following exercise is about self-love. Tim Stead (2018) describes it as a blessing to ourselves; I love that description. The words I have used below are taken from Tim's book, *See, Love, Be* (2018, p.109). The adult asks the children to do the following:

Sit with eyes closed, your hand on your heart and another hand on your belly.

Now repeat these words and keep repeating them for a few moments, allowing the words to sink in.

May I be safe
May I find peace
May I know kindness.

REFERENCES

Adams, I. (2010) *Cave Refectory Road*. London: Canterbury Press.

Brown, B. (2015) *Rising Strong*. London: Penguin.

Neff, K. (2011) *Self Compassion: Stop Beating Yourself Up and Leave Insecurity Behind*. New York: Harper Collins.

Stead, T. (2018) See, Love, Be: Mindfulness and the Spiritual life. London: SPCK.

CHAPTER 9

USING STORIES

Using stories is the most familiar way in which we work with children in the church. I love reading stories with children, and when my children were little, I particularly enjoyed sharing the Nick Butterworth and Mike Inkpen (1994) books of *Stories Jesus Told*. Often when we use stories in our church work it involves an adult telling a story, followed by a song about it and then a craft activity. This is okay, although it is a fairly formulaic template model. There are some more imaginative ways you can use stories and a few ideas follow.

STORY SACKS (ALL AGES)

Story sacks are commonly used in early years settings; they are a lovely way to share a story with a child and then open it up for them to explore through play. What I love about story sacks is that they encourage open-ended play. One way to use them is to read the story and then get the child to explore the story sack and play. The emphasis here is on the child directing the play; they may want to re-enact the story or take it another way, both are fine. This works best in a one-to-one situation or a small group. In the story sack you need objects that link to the story. The following is an example of what you might have in a story sack, but of course you can change it to suit your group.

You will need:

- *The House on the Rock* book
  (Butterworth and Inkpen 1994)
- toy figures of two men
- tub of sand
- small cake case to make a house in the sand
- tub of LEGO® bricks
- watering can containing water.

Read the story and then encourage the children to explore the story through the props provided in the story sack.

GODLY PLAY (ALL AGES)

There are training courses for using Godly Play and a UK website [1] dedicated to this. Many Church of England schools are now using Godly Play and a growing number of churches use it. There are resources you can buy and books about how to use Godly play. What I like about the approach is the way it promotes open-ended discussions and play; it is not prescriptive and

---

[1]   www.godlyplay.uk

it feels spacious. I also really appreciate that many of the resources are wooden, simple and beautiful. Godly Play shares a story through using different objects or images. It also uses secular resources that are linked to the theme. For example, if they are covering the Easter story they suggest children's books which link; not just Christian books, but children's story books drawing on the theme of bereavement. Godly Play sessions also use a variety of good art materials, for example, pastels, charcoal, chalk, pens and paper, enabling the children to respond creatively if they choose to. Some churches/ schools have a dedicated Godly Play room, where they are able to leave out resources and children can return to a story the following week.

To be able to deliver a Godly Play session, you need to know the story well to share it through the objects; this is not reading a story but using the ancient tradition of oral storytelling, with props to assist your storytelling. This is a very beautiful way of sharing a story: it is very spacious and un-rushed. It fits so well within a contemplative practice. To use this model you are encouraged to welcome children as they enter into the space. The children sit around in a circle, so all can see. The story is shared and then at the end 'I wonder' questions are used to encourage reflection and discussion. Children are then given time to respond and are able to choose whether they'd like to play with the storytelling materials, or respond by making art with a selection of different supplies.

For an example of how this works and further information there is a film on the Godly Play UK website.[2]

STATIONS SET UP TO PLAYFULLY EXPLORE A STORY

In the interview with Will and Esther in Chapter 2, they talk about using stations for children to explore a story. We used the idea of stations a lot in our Sanctuary services; Chapter 10 describes this more. The easiest way to describe them is as small areas/zones set up around a room, each one with a different activity to explore. By creating these zones you are enabling the group to reflect and engage in their own way. Stations often encourage a quiet, meditative way of engaging. As I have described in earlier chapters, stations are also a really good way of offering a layered approach for all ages. Below are some ideas of how you can use stories in a station format; again these are just ideas so do adapt them.

CREATION STORY (ALL AGES)

Start with the whole group together and tell them the creation story, either through reading, using images or using objects. Then encourage the group to explore the different stations. Have one station for each day. The aim of this is to keep each station very open ended: don't include instructions on what to do; allow the children to explore in whatever way they want. Some

---

[2]   www.godlyplay.uk/method

may want to spend all their time in one or two stations and others may want to try them all. Setting these up in tough spots on the floor can work really well (a tough spot is an early years description for a large builders tray – a very useful resource). Where possible offer multi-sensory items. You can use the ideas below or expand them to include your own ideas.

Day 1 – Let there be light
- dark material
- torches.

Day 2 – Let there be sky, land and sea
- blue material
- white material or cotton wool
- pot of soil
- pot of water
- pebbles
- stones.

Day 3– Let the land produce plants and trees
- pot of soil
- sticks with leaves on
- seeds/coffee beans/spices/dried rice
- flower heads
- leaves/herbs.

Day 4 – Let there be sun for the day and moon and stars for the night
- yellow/orange material
- white material
- dark material
- star shapes cut from foil.

Day 5– Let the water fill with creatures and the air with birds
- water in a large bowl
- toy sea creatures
- shells
- material for the sky
- toy birds.

Day 6 – Let the land fill with creatures and Adam and Eve to take care of the world
- a mix of toy land animals
- toy male and female characters
- pot of sand or soil
- pot of water.

By giving children time to explore these stations, you are giving them space to reflect and engage in the story. The act of engaging physically in the story can be very contemplative for children. It can also sometimes be more playful and that is fine.

At the end bring the group together and ask them for some thoughts about the story they have explored.

REFERENCE
Butterworth, N. and Inkpen, M. (1994) *The House on the Rock (Stories Jesus Told)*. London: Marshall Pickering.

CHAPTER 10

USING STATIONS

I have used the format of stations a lot with children; I find that they are a really useful way to create a space for children to be able to engage, reflect and participate at their level. There is often an open-ended structure to them, which encourages creativity. Stations can also be a useful tool to encourage a more reflective, contemplative space. They can be used for the whole session, or as one component of a session. Stations can be used with just children, with a mix of ages of children or with an all-age group.

As Sanctuary was an all-age community and all our services were all age, it was important that our services were accessible to everyone. We had a monthly cycle whereby we would meet once a month for a service, once a month for a discussion group and once a month for a community meal. Our approach was about stripping back the components of church and making it spacious and inclusive. In the majority of our services we used stations. We would often start a service together, sharing a reading linked to the theme of that service and an opening prayer, then we would all go and explore, engaging and participating with the stations. Our services were always run by a team of people, enabling different people to contribute, curate and bring ideas, and taking the burden off one person.

Stations are small areas/zones to explore and reflect on different themes/ideas. By using stations you are able to set them up in a way which works on different levels for different ages. There may be an activity to do that all ages can partake in, with words alongside for an older child or adult to reflect on. The encouragement behind these is to enable thinking, questioning and reflection rather than telling someone an answer.

Sometimes we curated a service based on one idea and would get everyone in the community to contribute something for a station or for the service. The Examen service, which I mentioned in Chapter 2, is an example of one these services. Below is the list of questions we used. In Chapter 2, I shared two of the examples my children did and in Chapter 7 I shared another example from this service, the prayer and felting exercise for 'What reached me today?'

THE EXAMEN: 'AT THE END OF THE DAY: A MIRROR OF QUESTIONS' (O'DONOHUE 2008, P.98)

- What dreams did I create last night?
- Where did my eyes linger today?
- Where was I blind?
- What did I learn today?
- What did I read?
- What new thoughts visited me?

- What differences did I notice in those closest to me?

- Who did I neglect?

- Where did I neglect myself?

- What did I begin today that might endure?

- How were my conversations?

- What did I do for the poor and excluded?

- Did I remember the dead today?

- Where could I have exposed myself to the risk of something different?

- Where did I allow myself to receive love?

- With whom today did I feel most myself?

- What reached me today? How deep did it imprint?

- Who saw me today?

- What visitations had I from the past and from the future?

- What did I avoid today?

- From the evidence – why was I given this day?

For the station 'Where did I remember the dead today?', my husband carved these words into a stone as if it was a memorial stone; he is letter cutter and stone carver by trade, so it fitted with his skills!

As part of the service we all explored and spent time with the stations. Some of the stations had things to do, others had space to reflect and think. All the stations enabled us to be contemplative.

This service was a good example of how an idea can work for different ages, with everyone in the community not only taking part in the service but also pulling it together, each creating a part. When we took this to Greenbelt and placed the stations around the Messy Space venue, which was family play space, we observed many people of different ages engaging in each of the stations. People were able to find their own moment of meeting with God, their own moment of stillness through exploring the questions.

REST SERVICE EXAMPLE

One of our services (written by me, Iain Cotton and Clare Birch) was on the theme of 'Rest'. We set up stations exploring this theme. Below are the stations we used and the words we used to go with them. The service was based on the passage:

> Are you tired? Worn out? Burned out on religion? Come to me. Get away with me and you'll recover your life. I'll show you how to take a real rest. Walk with me and work with me watch how I do it. Learn the unforced rhythms of grace. I won't lay anything heavy or ill-fitting on you. Keep company with me and you'll learn to live freely and lightly.
>
> (Matthew 11:28–30 MSG)

We started by reading this passage and then invited everyone to explore the stations. A list and descriptions of the stations are below.

HAMMOCK STATION

You will need:

- words printed out (see below)

- hammock with words written out next to it

- sensory pot plants around, for example, mint, lemon balm, lavender

- jug of cordial or water and glasses.

WORDS

'Are you tired? Worn out? Burned out on religion? Come to me. Get away with me and you'll recover your life.' (Matthew 11: 28–30 MSG)

Sometimes, just stopping is the hardest thing to do.

Hear the words of Jesus afresh today, and take some time to get away with Him.

Rest in the hammock and listen for His voice.

Take a sip of drink and reflect on the refreshment He promises.

Run your fingers through the herbs, smelling the different healing scents.

Allow yourself this time to stop, relax; just be, knowing you are in God's presence.

PLANTING STATION

You will need:

- words printed out (see below)
- compost
- beans
- small pots
- watering can.

WORDS

> Then Jesus said, 'God's kingdom is like seed thrown on a field by a man who then goes to bed and forgets about it. The seed sprouts and grows – he has no idea how it happens. The earth does it all without his help: first a green stem of grass, then a bud, then the ripened grain. When the grain is fully formed, he reaps – harvest time!'
>
> (Mark 4: 26–29 MSG)

Spend some time planting a bean. Take it home, water it, see it grow and then enjoy the food it produces.

Give thanks to God, who provides all that we need.

CLOTHES AND WELLIES STATION

You will need:

- words printed out (see below)
- gardening clothes of different sizes, for example, coat, waterproof trousers

- gardening gloves of different sizes
- wellies of different sizes.

WORDS

'Learn the unforced rhythms of grace. I won't lay anything heavy or ill-fitting on you. Keep company with me and you'll learn to live freely and lightly.' (Mark 4: 26–29 MSG)

How does it feel to put on someone else's clothes? Try on some of the gardener's garments. Are they too big? Too small? Comfortable or restricting?

These clothes are good for gardening in. They have a particular purpose for their owners. Outside that purpose they may seem ugly, uncomfortable and useless.

Think about your life today. Are there things in your life which feel heavy and ill-fitting? Roles which you have outgrown, or shoehorned yourself into through necessity or to meet the expectations of others?

Offer your thoughts and feelings to God.

His grace is for you today.

Ask Jesus to help you to learn how to keep company with Him, and to live freely and lightly, happy in your skin.

PRUNING STATION

You will need:

- words printed out (see below)

- secateurs
- branches to cut or a plant to cut back
- bin or compost bag.

WORDS

'Walk with me and work with me.' (Matthew 11: 28–30 MSG)

Gardeners know that although pruning looks destructive, it is often the only way to encourage and enable new growth. Without pruning, plants can become more prone to disease, produce fewer flowers and fruit, and have shorter lives.

Often we fear change and loss. They can be difficult and painful. We would rather hang on to what we know than let go and encounter the unknown. But just as with plants, this can hamper our growth and our fruitfulness.

How could you benefit from some pruning?

Do you need to cut away some areas of activity to enable new growth?

Spend some time thinking about this prayerfully before God; then take the secateurs and cut away a piece of the climber. Discard it in the bin provided.

As you are pruning, commit yourself to walking and working with God in this process of change and renewal.

SITTING STATION

You will need:

- words printed out (see below)
- small garden table
- two garden chairs.

WORDS

'Keep company with me and you'll learn to live freely and lightly.' (Matthew 11: 28–30 MSG)

Jesus invites you to join Him at the table. He welcomes you and wants to be with you.

Take this time to enjoy His presence, His welcome and His love for you.

DEN STATION

You will need:

- words printed out (see below)
- a pop-up tent or make a den out of clothes horse and blankets.

WORDS

'You who sit down in the High God's presence, Say this: "God, you're my refuge, I trust in you and I'm safe!"' (Psalm 91)

Give thanks to God for being your refuge, your safe place. If you are feeling scared or unsafe in any part of your life, lift these things to God and ask for His protection.

THOUGHTS ON THE 'REST' SERVICE

In this service we had toddlers, primary-aged children and teenagers taking part alongside the adults. The different activities in the services encouraged and enabled engagement at different levels. When you set up a service in this way, you notice some beautiful moments. I remember seeing one of the adults in our group lying in the hammock and child in the group pouring and offering them a drink. When children and adults are alongside one another, you often notice a playfulness in the adults that may not be there without the children. This style also allows adults who are not related to the children to engage with them in a gentle way; for example, another adult reading and explaining the words to a younger child.

I recognise that this style of doing worship will not suit everyone and that it can be very labour intensive; however, I wanted to include this chapter to show other ways you could try things. This style might be something you choose to do once a term or for Easter, Christmas or Harvest, for instance.

REFERENCE

O'Donohue, J. (2008) *To Bless the Space between Us: A Book of Blessings.* New York: Convergent Books.

CONCLUSION

I hope this book has given you some ideas and insights into how we can help children to engage in contemplative and stillness practice and why this is important for their wellbeing. I believe we are at a point in time when we need to teach children, from a young age, the tools which will aid them through life.

The ideas and practices in this book are meant to offer a starting point, a way into exploring this with children. I would encourage you to be curious and imaginative in these practices. So often the idea of contemplative practice can seem stuffy or something only for monastics. I really hope I have offered another way to view this and to see that we can open up these practices in a way which delights and is inviting to children.

Experiencing and practising contemplative stillness has been transformative for me; it has helped me to find a stillness and calmness that I badly needed. Over the years, and particularly for this book, I have been reading widely around this subject. There are many excellent writers who open up, explain, explore and help us to understand this ancient practice; I would encourage you to dip into some of the books I've referenced and especially those in the further reading list for Chapter 3.

Thank you for taking the time to read this book.

INDEX